HAPPY
RELATIONSHIPS

Also by Sam Owen

500 Relationships and Life Quotes

Resilient Me

Anxiety Free

HAPPY RELATIONSHIPS

7 Simple Rules to Create Harmony and Growth

Sam Owen

First published in Great Britain in 2020 by Orion Spring
an imprint of The Orion Publishing Group Ltd
Carmelite House, 50 Victoria Embankment
London EC4Y 0DZ

An Hachette UK Company

1 3 5 7 9 10 8 6 4 2

A CIP catalogue record for this book is
available from the British Library.

ISBN (Trade Paperback) 978 1 4091 7141 6
ISBN (eBook) 978 1 4091 7142 3

Typeset by Richard Carr

Printed and bound in Great Britain by Clays Ltd, Elcograf S.p.A.

MIX
Paper from
responsible sources
FSC® C104740

www.orionbooks.co.uk

To my amazing, loving, wise, charitable, strong, optimistic parents, Abdul Latif and Balqees Latif.

Contents

Part 1:
Happy Relationships, Happy Life

Your Relationships, Your Mental Health, Your Happiness

'Life without love is like a tree without blossoms or fruit.'
Kahlil Gibran

Hayley used to dream about having a husband, home and children of her own, but she only ever seems to find herself single – again. It's always the guy who ends the relationship, and now she's worried whether something is intrinsically wrong with her. 'Actually, maybe I don't want to be with someone after all!' she thinks, fooling herself, because the reality is starting to hurt and she's beginning to lose hope of achieving her relationship and family goals.

Stewart had been happily married until his wife told him, unexpectedly, that she had been seeing someone else and didn't know whether she wanted to stay or leave. He had thought they would grow old together; now he finds his self-esteem slipping daily and feels like he is being sucked into the ground. He knows he needs to accept reality and move on, but he's struggling to. His self-care is at an all-time low, along with his self-worth.

Mo, on the other hand, is kind and charismatic and has been excelling in his job for years, but now, with a new boss renowned for being culturally insensitive and somewhat unpleasant in general, Mo begins to worry about his prospects for a major promotion he has been working towards for a year.

Then there's Jenny. Sweet Jenny struggles to connect with her parents and dreads phone calls and visiting them. 'They are always critical of every decision I make,' she thinks to herself. 'They only worry about how my achievements reflect on them, how me being divorced affects their reputation, and they frequently look at me with patronising eyes and tell me I am making the wrong decisions. I hate how they make me feel every time we connect, yet I have to connect otherwise they guilt-trip me into feeling like a selfish daughter.' Jenny desperately wants a happy, healthy relationship with them, she just doesn't know how, or whether it's even possible.

All four have concerns about their respective relationships and their concerns make them question themselves. The heartache leads to self-doubt and sometimes self-sabotage, as well as concerns about their future. This isn't how all people handle such challenges, though. The person who has a positive relationship with themselves, and a positive relationship with everyone else in their life, significant and less significant, is resilient to the aggression and accusations others can throw at them. They stand tall, knowing who they are at their core: worthy of love and good fortune, not representative of the false accusations others may make, and undeserving of the aggression they may be receiving. The hurtful attacks from others bounce off them over and over again because they have a healthy self-esteem and good people in their life to hold them up and protect them, even when there is a barrage of aggression coming their way, as might be the case with the victim of a psychologically abusive partner or a psychopathic boss. This is why, to have happy, healthy relationships in your life, it's essential that **you are happy and healthy within** and **surround yourself with positive relationships**.

In my coaching practice, I have seen both sides of the coin. The people who don't have happy relationships with themselves and others often begin to cave (at least until I've helped them to prop themselves back up again), while those who do are defiant, resilient and resolute no matter what agony they're facing, which is always heart-warming and impressive to watch. All I ever want for my clients is to help them become happy and healthy and able to achieve their important goals. I am known for helping my clients overcome long-standing, chronic issues in their life, usually in just two to six coaching sessions – issues they would ordinarily require a much lengthier counselling/therapy programme for – and their success ultimately comes down to them taking charge of their life in small, significant ways and doing so consistently, which is exactly what I'm going to show you how to do. So, as you read on, know that I am going to help you change your attitude to yourself and your relationships, taking them from where they are now to where you want them to be, and I'll do this by suggesting **small, simple, significant changes** that you can **apply consistently** to your life. Many of these tweaks feel good, too, so they will help you stay in charge of your relationships, happiness and health.

This book covers good habits that you will want to implement daily, near daily or weekly, in order to reap the rewards you're looking for, and most of them will just be little tweaks to how you currently think and behave. At the end of the book I will show you how to create a personalised

4 week plan that incorporates these rewarding tweaks into your daily/weekly habits, so that by the end of the four weeks, you'll have a significantly happier relationship with yourself and others. When you commit to four weeks of consistent changes, you'll notice your relationship with yourself and others transform, and when that happens, you'll naturally maintain those habits. In the future, if you slip by accident, you'll notice, and then you'll just need to remember which habits were proven to help you and start doing them again.

I'm guessing you have picked up this book because you are in a difficult place. I'm really sorry you're going through this emotional pain. Thank you for entrusting me with the privilege of helping you. I will do my utmost to help you move from where you are now to the place you want and deserve to be. All you need to do now is become a serious student of your own life. *Do not* hurt yourself emotionally or physically (more on this later) and maintain hope; we're going to get you through this and guide you to a good place – a place of owning your worth and taking charge of your relationships, your happiness, your mental and physical health – by **ensuring that your future only consists of people who truly love you and have the right to be in your life**. Not everyone gets a pass to access your life; only you can decide who does.

So sit back, relax and have a notepad and pen handy for jotting down any important thoughts and ideas as you read on. Be kind to yourself and be proud of yourself for taking this step to making many positive changes in your relationships and, ultimately, in every other part of your life.

People Power

'Humans need others to survive. Regardless of one's sex, country or culture of origin, or age or economic background, social connection is crucial to human development, health and survival,' conclude researchers.[1]

Let's be clear, though: some relationships are not good for our health, happiness and longevity. Fact. A wealth of research demonstrates how negative relationships can damage our health and that feeling lonely can actually shorten our lifespan;[2] it also shows that people with good-quality, close relationships and those who feel well connected with other human beings are happier, physically healthier and live longer.[3,4] So if, after wholeheartedly embracing the principles and techniques in this book, and getting additional professional help if required, you recognise that it's time to walk away, then please make sure you do. Sometimes you can spend years doing everything in your power to make something right, but it takes two people on the same wavelength to make any kind of relationship successful, and if only one person is putting the effort in, it won't work – no matter how much you have loved them with your words and actions.'

Your Happiness Is Our Happiness

The other thing we all must recognise is that how each individual feels has an impact on mankind. Human emotions are contagious, both online and offline. Research suggests that happiness[5] and depressive symptoms[6] can be transferred from one person to their friends, their friends' friends and their friends' friends' friends – in other words, emotions can spread to and from people well beyond their own immediate social network. This means we are not only affected by what is happening to us; we are affected by what is happening to others, sometimes thousands of miles away. But even closer to home, your friends, family and colleagues don't want to see you hurting; out of compassion for you, and because it affects them, too. So getting yourself to a happy and healthy place is important for you, and important for the rest of mankind, too. We are all connected. We rise together, we fall together. There is no 'them and us' – we're in this world together. Don't let politics and propaganda fool you. Don't let hate groups confuse you. We are one. So let's make a happy and healthier world together, and that starts with us as individuals. Now my fellow sweet human, let's talk about what you came here for: you, your relationships, your happiness.

Three Pillars of Happy Relationships

'However successful you are, there is no substitute
for a close relationship. We all need them.'
Francesca Annis

For a relationship between any two people to survive and thrive, both people need to honour the following Three Pillars of Happy Relationships:

1. Be happy and healthy within

2. Be authentic

3. Be proactive

When even one person in the relationship isn't adhering to these pillars, the relationship will not survive, regardless of how much the other person is honouring them.

It can sometimes be hard to realise that the other person isn't as committed as you are. Don't feel bad for overlooking things because your judgement was clouded by:

◊ your deep love for them;

◊ your desire and intention to stay in a relationship with them;

◊ your belief in their false promises to you (including marriage vows to be together until death parts you or other major words or gestures of love);

◊ the lies they may have told you (and even themselves);

◊ their perhaps believable excuses for behaving the way they do;

◊ their addiction to drugs or other distractions that they insisted were simply a pastime;

◊ the many good times that you have shared and continue to share that overshadowed the bad.

Sometimes, we want a relationship to work so much, and expect it to work so much, that we completely miss the red flags, however astute we normally are at spotting red flags of any kind! Such is the power of love; it can blind us. What's so interesting is that when you yourself are loving, compassionate and committed, you can end up filling in the gaps in their love, thereby not noticing that they are not treating you as you treat them.

When the Three Pillars of Happy Relationships are present, you can feel the calm inside your body and other people can sense it, helping you to connect and bond with your fellow humans. When the Three Pillars of Happy Relationships are not present, you can feel uneasy inside and other people can sense that, too, hindering you from connecting and bonding. People may not know what they're picking up; they just know they feel an awkwardness in your presence, because we humans are smart like that, wired that way, whether they can put their finger on what it is or not.

So let's look at what happens when the Three Pillars of Happy Relationships are present (i.e. you're happy and healthy within, authentic and proactive) and what happens when you are none of those things.

When the Three Pillars of Happy Relationships are present:

◊ You **feel calm, resilient, valuable, energetic** and **confident**, and you **exude sincerity**, so you find it easier to connect with others and others find it easier to connect with you.

◊ Consequently, **you ensure you only keep people in your life who deserve a place there** and you surround yourself with those who reinforce your resilience, well-being and self-esteem, thereby helping you to also achieve your important life goals.

◊ And because you **take responsibility** for what's not working by consistently making positive changes, you're able to overcome any issues or, at the very least, recognise when it's time to walk away.

When the Three Pillars of Happy Relationships are not present:

◊ You **feel uneasy, overwhelmed, fragile, fatigued, lacking in worth and insecure,** and you **channel awkwardness.** As such, you find it more difficult to connect with others and others find it more difficult to connect with you.

◊ Consequently, **you allow people into your life who do not deserve a place there** and you accidentally surround yourself with those who erode your resilience, well-being and self-esteem, thereby also hindering you from achieving your important life goals.

◊ And because you **evade responsibility**, you let problems continue and deepen and threaten your relationship, and often don't have the clarity or confidence to recognise when it is time to walk away.

I want to help you honour these Three Pillars of Happy Relationships every single day, so I've designed 7 Simple Rules to Create Harmony and Growth. As we go through the book, we'll look at each of the rules in turn, and think about how you can apply them to your relationships:

1. Create helpful thoughts.

2. Love and look after yourself.

3. Be a friend.

4. Communicate well.

5. Nurture the good, prune the bad.

6. Achieve personal goals.

7. Problem-solve relentlessly.

In each of these seven chapters you'll find insights, research that highlights the importance of each rule and simple strategies that allow you to easily implement them into your life. Remember, you'll achieve happy relationships by changing your bad relationship habits into good relationship habits. First, let's take a look at how you can do a quick self-assessment, any time, any place, so that you know if you and your relationships are on the right track.

Self-Assessment Leads
to Self-Awareness

'Listen to your intuition. It will tell you
everything you need to know.'
Anthony J. D'Angelo

When it comes to understanding yourself and making good decisions, there is one tool that will help you more than any other: your body. When you proactively tune in to your body, you notice visceral sensations generated by the processes automatically taking place inside it, such as fluctuations in your heartbeat's rhythm and strength, your breathing, sensations of internal tension, sensations of internal relaxation, and so on.

Human intuition works by the brain scanning and evaluating information captured through the senses, consciously and subconsciousl,[7] information stored in memory,[8] and pattern identification[9] and intuitive hunches can be the result of these joined-up calculations.[10] Intuition is your ability to understand or know something instinctively, without conscious reasoning. It allows you to access information that your brain and body know subconsciously but that you don't yet know consciously. To gauge what your subconscious knows before it reaches your conscious mind, you can take signals from your body's physiological reactions, which will help you to make the right decisions. For example, does this person seem trustworthy? Are there any inconsistencies in what this person is saying and doing? Should I pursue career A or B? Will I have a rigorous workout if I go to the gym right now? Should I tell my friend about X or not? And so on. You might find that your heart begins to beat harder or that you feel tension in your upper back or your stomach feels tense, suggesting this is perhaps a bad sign or decision for you. On the other hand, the absence of such signs, or a relaxed body as you consider one particular option over several others, may help indicate the opposite – that this may be a good sign or decision for you. Your telltale signs will be specific to you. Therefore, it can be useful to intercept this information so that you don't have to wait for it to reach your consciousness – which can take time that you may not have – and you can use your body to help you do so. Often, you can just decide: does this option or decision make me 'feel good' or 'feel bad'? When you 'feel good', aside from your body feeling relaxed and void of tension, you may also experience a bodily feeling of calm or lightness. When you 'feel bad', aside from your bodily sensation of tension and lack of inner calm, you may experience it as agitation or heaviness.

⊨ OVER TO YOU ⊨

Tune in to Your Intuition

When you want to decipher which decision is right for you – whether you have multiple options to choose from or a relationship to pursue or distance yourself from – use the following tips to help you tune in to your intuition and make great decisions quickly and easily.

Relax yourself and quiet your mind, as it's usually difficult to tune in to your intuition when you are stressed and distracted. For example, light some candles, go for a brisk walk, have a hot soak in the bath.

Focus your heart and mind on the thing you want answers to, so you can tune in to the feeling. Think of it like focusing your eyesight on something far away or listening closely for something.

Very often it's the first answer that pops into your head before you've had time to consciously over-think or even finish asking yourself the question, that is the right one! The answer rapidly flashes through your mind and feels detached from your conscious evaluation process.

Use bodily sensations to establish how you feel about each possible option you're considering. For example, let's assume you need to make a decision and you have three options to choose from, X, Y and Z:

- Imagine yourself pursuing one of the three possible options.

- As you wholeheartedly imagine pursuing that option, pay attention to the sensations you feel within your body.

- Repeat this exercise for each of the three options.

- You'll usually find that one of the options triggers the most relaxed feeling compared with the other options as you vividly imagine each one separately. The presence of a relaxed state is a good indicator of which decision may be the right one for you. The presence of tension is a good sign that something may not be right for you.

- The internal bodily sensations may be felt around your chest, back, neck, shoulders, scalp, stomach or elsewhere. Your most obvious telltale-sign regions will be specific to you. Certainly, though, the heart area is a useful one to tune in to, as you can sometimes detect beat-to-beat changes. Also pay attention to general tension and relaxation, which can help direct you towards the right decision.

- Consider the physiological response as your subconscious mind's way of telling you, 'I've scanned all the information, stored and new, and I suggest that option X is safe or right for you and that option Y is unsafe or wrong for you.' When you have the courage to follow your gut feeling, watch how hours, days or weeks later your conscious mind delivers the specific reasons that support your intuitive hunch.

Use common sense when applying these tips. If you're feeling tense about something, use conscious reasoning and questions to decipher if the tension is due to your anxiety about doing something new (e.g. asking someone out on a date) or due to the option being fraught with problems (e.g. you don't feel in the right place to date right now).

Intuition is scientifically recognised, and when you use yours, you give yourself access to information that will help you make good decisions effortlessly.

Tuning in to your body is also a great way to understand what you're thinking and feeling right now. Sports coaches sometimes use what are known as biofeedback methods with world-class athletes to help them see **the impact of thoughts and emotions on their internal physiology and neurology**. They might do this by measuring heart-rate variability (HRV) and brainwaves, for example.[11] By making a person aware of the negative impact of their thoughts and emotions, they are motivated to change how they think and behave – they might focus on more positive thoughts and use slower, steadier breathing in order to calm the mind. It also allows them to see how different mental states affect their brainwaves – these biofeedback methods are able to show how negatively stress and a lack of concentration can affect a person, in comparison to someone who feels calm and focused. While you may not have access to biofeedback equipment to measure your HRV or brainwaves, you do still have your own in-built biofeedback monitors: your bodily sensations. When you turn your focus inwards towards these feelings, you begin to notice your heart rate, heartbeat strength, muscle tension or relaxation, your breathing and sweating. Understanding these will help you to adjust your thoughts and behaviours. Simply **tune in** to what your bodily sensations are telling you about your emotional state. Are you feeling anxious, calm, panicky, confident, tense, relaxed, sad, happy? **Work out** which thoughts the feeling relates to and what sort of decision it suggests you need to make. For example, does it mean you are too overwhelmed to say 'yes' to more work, or that you still don't know how to have that awkward conversation with your friend when you meet him tonight? Or that you need to get out and meet more people so that you feel less isolated? Bodily sensations can tell us a lot about the nature of our current thoughts and emotions.

So now you are armed with a way of understanding how to tap in to your current thoughts, feelings and intuition, let's explore the 7 Simple Rules to Create Harmony and Growth, which will help you to honour the Three Pillars of Happy Relationships:

1. Be happy and healthy within

2. Be authentic

3. Be proactive

SUMMARY

Own your worth so that others see it, too. Be true to who you are deep inside and do your best to make your relationships as healthy as they can be. If they don't work out, learn from them and go on to have better future relationships. It matters to you, your loved ones and mankind.

You're just looking for the people you click with; either you do or you don't. It's not that you're not good enough, it's that the connection between you isn't energetic enough.

Part 2:
7 Simple Rules to Create Harmony and Growth

Rule #1: Create Helpful Thoughts

*'Such as are your habitual thoughts, such also will be the
character of your mind; for the soul is dyed by the thoughts.'*
Marcus Aurelius

Our thoughts tell our brain what to notice, what to focus on,
how to feel emotionally and physically, and what to do. As
such, our thoughts steer the direction our lives are going in,
each moment of each day.

There is a wealth of research that highlights the importance
of focusing your mind on positive thoughts and avoiding
negative ones. For example, repetitive negative thinking such
as worry and rumination have been linked to mood disorders
such as anxiety and depression, [12] and self-critical thoughts
have been linked to anxiety, [13] low self-esteem, depressive
symptoms and eating disorders. [14] Gratitude, where you
habitually focus your thoughts on the things you appreciate
about your life, has on the other hand been linked to a
reduction in stress and depressive symptoms, [15] and an improved
quality of life, directly and also indirectly, by lowering perceived
stress and improving mental health. [16] In other research,
gratitude has been linked to improved physical health. [17]
Meanwhile, having an optimistic frame of mind has been
shown to positively impact the recovery of patients who have

suffered from acute coronary syndrome. [18] Brief expressions of gratitude have been shown to leave lasting effects on neural activity in the medial prefrontal cortex as much as three months later, which really highlights the ongoing effects of your old thoughts on your present brain. [19] So negative and positive thoughts impact your mental health, your physical health and your emotional well-being.

You cannot leave negative thoughts on autopilot. If you do, they will completely unravel your relationships, your happiness, your health and your life. And it doesn't even matter whether the thoughts you think are true or not; they will still affect your perspective, emotions, behaviours, relationships and life as whole. Let's use a silly example to really show that our thoughts influence our lives.

Imagine for a moment that you think all cats are highly dangerous animals:

◊ Would you avoid domesticated cats in close proximity to you?

◊ Would you experience anxiety and/or fear when you were near domesticated cats?

◊ If you were dining outdoors in the summer, would you struggle to enjoy your meal if a neighbour's cat kept wandering about by your table?

Of course you will have answered yes, yes and yes, because you intuitively understood that these would be natural reactions if you viewed all cats as highly dangerous animals. In your mind, your safety is being threatened, even if in reality you can read that example and know that it isn't.

Is the reality shaping your reaction in this scenario, or your thoughts? Your thoughts: because the reality is that all cats are not highly dangerous animals, but if your personal outlook states that they are, you will respond accordingly, regardless of the reality.

To help you experience first-hand how your own thoughts are shaping your life, let's look at what happens when you have positive thoughts and what happens when you have negative thoughts. In coaching, I use this alternative version of Cognitive Behavioural Therapy's Hot Cross Bun (Five Areas) Model called the Thought–Feedback Cycle (see diagrams below and overleaf). This helps clients to understand exactly how their thoughts or outlooks affect their life.

Hot Cross Bun Model (CBT)

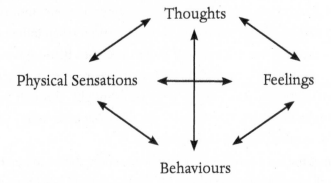

Thoughts

Physical Sensations   Feelings

Behaviours

Thought–Feedback Cycle

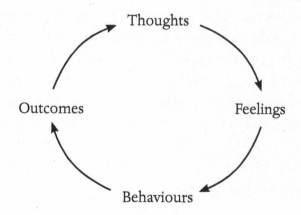

The Thought–Feedback Cycle illustrates how our thoughts (which are in our control) influence our emotions, our emotions then influence our behaviours, those behaviours then influence the outcomes we achieve, and those outcomes then influence our subsequent thoughts. Let's use an example to see what happens when you run a negative thought through the Thought–Feedback Cycle and then what happens when you run a positive thought through it.

Imagine for a moment that Rita repeatedly thinks to herself that she is unlikely to find her Mr Right to spend her life with, versus thinking that she is absolutely going to find her Mr Right to spend her life with:

Thoughts/Outlook:	Rita holds the thought (outlook) that she is unlikely to find her Mr Right	Rita holds the thought (outlook) that she is absolutely going to find her Mr Right
Behaviours: How many hours might Rita spend proactively searching for Mr Right?	An hour or so a month, or just minutes each month	Several hours a week or several hours a month
Emotions: How might Rita react if asked on a date by a seemingly nice, genuine person?	Cynicism and/or anxiety	Excitement and/or optimism
Outcomes: How likely is it that Rita still won't have found her Mr Right three years from now?	Likely or highly likely	Unlikely or highly unlikely

Over-simplified? Yes, but you get the gist. The example illustrates the effect our thoughts have on our emotions and behaviours and, thus, the outcomes we achieve in life.

Notice how:

- Negative thoughts lead to **self-sabotaging and goal-sabotaging** emotions and behaviours that will eventually sabotage your chance of happiness in life.

- Positive thoughts lead to **self-serving and goal-serving** emotions and behaviours and thus serve your goals in life.

We attach thoughts to things every day, throughout the day. We don't often think about the ways in which our thoughts are shaping how the present moment is unfolding, but they do. Thoughts shape your life. They influence what you notice, how you feel, how you behave and your future thoughts.

Now try it for yourself using the quick exercise opposite.

⊨ OVER TO YOU ⊨

Understanding the Effects Thoughts Have on Your Life

Run one of your frequently occurring negative thoughts through the Thought–Feedback Cycle by completing the statements on the left:

A frequently occurring negative thought I have is ...	e.g. my partner doesn't understand me.
The emotions/feelings I subsequently experience as a result of those negative thoughts are ...	e.g. sad, frustrated and anxious.
The behaviours I subsequently indulge in as a result of those negative emotions/ feelings are ...	e.g. I talk less about my concerns and spend more time alone.
The outcomes I subsequently achieve as a result of such behaviours are ...	e.g. our relationship problems fester and we become more distant from one another.
The subsequent thoughts I then have that feed back into my emotions as the cycle continues are ...	e.g. my partner doesn't understand me and doesn't seem to care about us.

⊨══⊨

Now that you know your thoughts – which are under your control – are affecting every moment of your life, let's think about how your thoughts are affecting your relationships with yourself and others.

Thoughts About Yourself, Thoughts About Others, Thoughts About Life

While negative thoughts such as worry have been repeatedly linked to poor mental and physical health, research also finds that talking positively to ourselves about our wants and desires moves us in the direction of our goals, [20, 21] for example, telling yourself, 'I feel confident in meetings'; 'I look after my mind and body'; 'I always find solutions, quickly' can actually help those statements come true.

Now imagine how your current thoughts are shaping your self-image, self-esteem and relationships. Bearing in mind the Thought–Feedback Cycle, and the effects your thoughts naturally have on your emotions, behaviours and outcomes, think about how the following thoughts would, and may well be, influencing the outcomes you achieve:

◊ I'm ugly and fat.

◊ I don't deserve to have nice things.

◊ I only ever date people who mess me around.

◊ All my friends are too busy to spend time with me.

◊ I have to look after my family first. My happiness is not important.

◊ My girlfriend/boyfriend takes me for granted.

◊ My neighbours are a constant nightmare.

◊ My boss doesn't like me.

◊ I'm rubbish at my job.

Now imagine how differently these thoughts would steer your emotions, behaviours and outcomes if you instead affirmed the positive opposite:

◊ I'm attractive and confident.

◊ I deserve to have nice things.

◊ I only ever date people who treat me well.

◊ All my friends make time for me.

◊ I have to look after myself and my family. My happiness is important, too.

◊ My girlfriend/boyfriend appreciates me.

◊ My neighbours are pleasant enough.

◊ My boss likes me.

◊ I'm great at my job.

Thinking positive statements – whether they're currently true or not – will have an effect on your emotions and behaviours and achievements. So it's up to you to choose your words wisely. Only you can do that. Only you can know which specific thoughts will positively impact you, but you will reap massive rewards when you do.

Right from the early days of my coaching practice, I witnessed my clients reporting back improvements in their marriages, their dating lives and their relationships with their children and parents, as well as in their energy, mental clarity, self-esteem, mental health and well-being – all because they'd simply taken charge of replacing frequent negative thoughts with frequent positive ones, allowing them to become happy and healthy within (Happy Relationships Pillar 1) and much more proactive (Happy Relationships Pillar 3).

So from now on, when you think about yourself and your worth, and when you think about others and what you want from your relationships with them, you have to ensure that your thoughts are taking you in the direction you want to go. The way to do this is to start with the end in mind, i.e. what do I want and what sort of language will direct my mind to help me achieve it? I have included more on how to do this in the coming pages.

Let's say you want to have a healthier relationship with your mother, but you don't know how. You question if she even loves you, though deep down you believe she must, even if it is in her own peculiar way. Now, you have a choice here about how you use your thoughts and what you tell your brain to pay attention to and work towards, consciously and subconsciously. You can focus primarily on what you don't like and on what the problems are: 'My mum doesn't love me and nothing I ever do is good enough.' Or you can focus on what you would like and finding solutions, e.g. 'My mum loves me in her own way, and I'll work out how to build a better relationship with her, where she respects me and is proud of me.' By the very nature of the instructions you are feeding your brain, it's clear that the former self-talk will create negative emotions such as disempowerment and despondency, while the latter self-talk will create positive emotions such as empowerment and hopefulness. These negative emotions will result in self-sabotaging and goal-sabotaging behaviours such as poor self-care and unnecessary arguments; the positive emotions will result in self-serving and goal-serving behaviours such as good self-care and conflict-free communication. Consequently, the negative thoughts will ultimately result in driving a further distance between you and your mother, while the positive thoughts, which lead to positive behaviours, will ultimately help you bridge the gap between you and your mother. Always focus your mind on the direction in which you want to travel.

Steer your life away from your fears and dislikes and towards your goals and desires by choosing your thoughts and words wisely. Think of your thoughts as though they are your hands on the steering wheel of your life, moving left, right, going straight, avoiding potholes and ditches and honking the horn occasionally.

And if you do find yourself getting stuck in one of the potholes (i.e. you find yourself obsessing over thoughts that are making you feel miserable) then distract yourself with an exercise that instantly transforms your thoughts – and therefore your emotions and behaviours – from negative and self-sabotaging to positive and helpful. You might find one of the self-care or happiness-boosting strategies in the next chapter useful, or you might just put on a song or three that always makes you feel good, recall a certain happy memory (e.g. your wedding day, a family holiday, a funny incident with a friend), look at images that uplift you (such as cute animals or nature or your own photographs of good times you've had) or immerse yourself in a book or TV show.

Now, let's put you in charge of your daily thinking habits, too. To work out what you need to say to yourself, use the method on page 35 for replacing negative thoughts and self-talk with positive thoughts and self-talk. The thoughts and words you speak form the starting point of your current and future achievements. That's you in the driving seat of your life, hands on the steering wheel. Steer your life to where you truly want to go, not to where you're scared to stay or go.

⊨ OVER TO YOU ⊨

Create a Habit of Talking Positively to Yourself

Whether you're sabotaging your relationships or self-esteem with your negative thinking or whether your negative thoughts are directly sabotaging your ability to be happy and healthy within, authentic and proactive (the Three Pillars of Happy Relationships), ensure that you talk to yourself as you would want a best friend to talk to you. As a simple rule:

- If it's negative, deflates you, knocks your self-worth, self-esteem, confidence or relationships, and/or sounds like something a non-well-wisher would say, don't say it. Would you want your best friend, someone who is looking out for your happiness, to say it to you?

- If it's positive, nourishes your self-worth, self-esteem, confidence or relationship, and/or sounds like something a best friend would say, say it.

Use the following steps to help:

1. List any negative statements you frequently say to yourself that sabotage your self-esteem, relationships, happiness, health and your goals. Then stop saying them. It's as simple as that. As you identify more, ban them, too.

2. Make a habit of talking positively to yourself ALL the time. Every time you catch yourself thinking something negative, turn the thought around. Do something often enough and

it becomes a habit (more on this on pages 119–125).

3. Use affirmations to help you. Affirmations are positive
   statements spoken in the present tense that help you to focus
   your mind on the necessary thoughts, qualities, emotions and
   behaviours you need to achieve happy relationships, healthy
   self-esteem and any other goals you may have.

   a. Affirmations should create inner ease rather than inner
      unease. So if you are affirming 'I feel confident' and this
      is creating inner unease, temporarily affirm, 'I am
      becoming increasingly confident every day,' and then,
      once your confidence has grown, thanks to your self-
      talk and the ensuing emotions and behaviours, then you
      can affirm, 'I feel confident.' Your bodily sensations and
      inner critic will instantly tell you if something feels
      comfortable or not, so use those to inform your
      affirmation-creation process.

   b. Create your affirmations in the present tense to reflect
      that you already think a certain way and/or already
      possess certain qualities, for example:

      • 'I have mental clarity.' (Or 'I have increasing mental
        clarity,' rather than, 'I want mental clarity.')
      • 'I am capable of achieving anything I set my mind to.'
      • 'I am compassionate and patient with myself and
        others.'
      • 'I am skilled at resolving relationship problems.'
      • 'I always find solutions quickly.'
      • 'I look after my mind and body.'
      • 'I communicate well with my loved ones.'

4. You want to make a habit of talking to yourself in a helpful, goal-serving way so that positive statements become part of your routine. Therefore, affirm these statements as often as you can, but at least first thing in the morning and last thing at night, repeating each one a few times, as desired. The former will help set up your day with a goal-serving focus. The latter will help you to absorb the affirmation in your relaxed state, and given that the brain problem-solves while we sleep (as we'll see later on) and that new information combines with memories to help us make great intuitive decisions, you can go to sleep with these positive statements fresh in your mind, allowing your brain to problem-solve how you can become or achieve those things.

Your Thoughts Affect Your Self-Image and Self-Esteem

Research also finds that self-compassion – which stems from thinking kindly towards yourself and allowing yourself to make mistakes – is linked to feelings of well-being, particularly in older adults, and to better self-esteem and less of a tendency to depression, regardless of age. [22]

Given that your thoughts determine what you notice, how you behave, what you consciously and subconsciously work towards, and the outcomes you achieve, it's essential that you think kindly of yourself, always boosting your self-image and self-esteem. Stop saying negative things about your abilities and your worth, whether you think they are true or not, and stop reliving incidents when you 'messed up' in some way, because, as we've seen, you'll work towards whichever you frequently affirm and you'll find 'proof' of whatever you focus on, whether it's real or imagined. Change your thoughts and you change your life.

Perhaps you recognise some of your own thinking patterns in some of these negative statements:

◊ I am stupid.

◊ Nobody will ever love me.

◊ Why would anyone want to be my friend?

◊ There's nothing I am good at.

◊ I always screw up.

◊ People don't take me seriously.

Stop saying those things to yourself, right now. Just stop. You're not doing yourself any favours and you're not doing anyone else any favours either ... unless they are the kind of people who want to see others unhappy, struggling, failing. If you have people like that near your life or in it, don't help them to unravel your happiness, health, relationships and successes. Do the opposite. Make your thoughts about yourself positive so that you elevate and maintain a healthy self-image and healthy self-esteem by ensuring your mind works at it, consciously and subconsciously, every minute of every day.

And just to give you an idea of how powerfully effective holding a negative self-image is when it comes to unravelling your relationships and self-esteem,[23] one study found that doing so while having a conversation with someone (a) makes an already anxious person feel more anxious, (b) makes them behave in ways that make it more difficult to build a relationship with someone (such as avoiding eye contact), (c) makes them think they have come across worse than they have and (d) does actually negatively affect how others perceive and experience them. [24] So watch how you think about yourself. Cut out the self-criticising and self-bullying. Talk to yourself only as you would expect a loving friend to speak to you and you will build better relationships more easily and bolster your self-esteem. Don't make your fears a reality; make your positive goals a reality.

One of my young clients, Gerrard, came to see me because he was feeling anxious and other talking therapies weren't helping him. In our first session he told me that he was struggling to make friends at university, and this was creating significant anxiety, so much so that his studies were now being affected. Gerrard was an otherwise bright student, but his grades were slipping and so was his self-esteem. He felt lonely and was questioning his religious beliefs, his familial relationships, whether he would ever make friends, whether there was simply something wrong with him – all sorts – in a bid to understand himself and the predicament he found himself in.

What transpired in that first session was that his self-image (how he thought about himself) was impacting how he was feeling and behaving around others. He worried that people didn't take him seriously, and never would. This thought process then led to the fixation that people would never make an effort to befriend him, as they 'never did', and that he would forever be lonely, all of which exacerbated the anxiety. As he was assuming that others his age didn't want to be friends with him, he behaved in ways that told people he wasn't interested in them. As a result, he came across as aloof, suggesting to potential new friends that he was not open to the idea of friendship. He wouldn't initiate conversations – instead, his body would be turned away from people who tried to talk to him, while he maintained a serious gaze, with no smiling. In short, he gave no verbal or non-verbal signs that he would welcome friendship. The reality was, he was letting his negative self-image, and his negative thoughts about others, sabotage him far more than the reality itself was doing. Once I had helped him to replace his negative self-image with a positive one, his emotions and behaviours changed, and he managed to completely eliminate the anxiety. Without those self-sabotaging and goal-sabotaging thoughts, he felt calm and confident, behaved authentically (Happy Relationships Pillar 2), became proactive (Happy Relationships Pillar 3) and built relationships easily. By becoming happy and healthy within (Happy Relationships Pillar 1), he was able to forge happy relationships with others.

SUMMARY

Thoughts steer the direction your life is travelling in and they determine the health and well-being of your relationships with yourself and others. How you repeatedly think becomes a habit, one that will either serve your relationship goals or sabotage them, so choose thoughts that will help rather than hinder your health, happiness and relationships.

Rule #2: Love and
Look After Yourself

*There are two ways you can live life: what looks good
to others or what is good for you.*

Loving and looking after yourself is a full-time job – have no illusions about it. You must balance this responsibility with all the other responsibilities you have in your life. When your health or well-being are off balance, your life will be, too, and this will usually affect your relationships. Sure, relationships, careers, health, social lives, hobbies and interests can handle a bit of neglect from time to time – hopefully they are resilient enough to withstand a little erosion – but over an extended period of time, that erosion weakens them, and sometimes holes will form. It's through those gaps that elements of our life might fall.

Self-care – via your thoughts and actions – tells your brain how much you value yourself, thereby shaping your self-esteem and overall well-being on a daily basis. It also gives you the energy to deal with life. Abandon your self-care and you eventually lose energy and resilience. Then you might think, 'I'm not very good at my job, I'm never going to get that promotion', or 'I find my partner draining', or 'I am getting old', or 'I'm becoming lazy.' Actually, maybe you just need to look after yourself more. Maybe the rest of your life would still feel satisfying and you would still be an active go-getter, if only you were rested, nourished and re-charged enough.

There are two areas you need to tend to: your mind and your body. Do this daily and you'll help ensure you are happy and healthy within (Happy Relationships Pillar 1) and maintain a healthy self-image and self-esteem.

Mind

We started addressing the mind in the previous chapter. First, the mind needs to be nourished with realistic, positive thoughts; thoughts about yourself that help you to feel and be your best and achieve your goals, and thoughts that help your relationships with others to be their best. Second, the mind must also not be overloaded too often with too much information. How much is too much is specific to each individual, and by tuning in, you can work out when you've hit your peak and know that it's time to take the load off, at least for a short time, while you replenish your resilience reserves. Third, the mind also pays attention to how you're letting the people in your life treat you. We'll cover this latter topic in detail when we look at Happy Relationships Rule #5: Nurture the Good, Prune the Bad (page 127).

Body

The body must be cared for, too. As Jim Rohn said, 'Take care of your body. It's the only place you have to live.' Looking after yourself physically is not only how you survive, but also how you stay fit and healthy, allowing you to thrive in life and in your relationships. Then there is the mind–body connection, which means that how we treat our body can impact our mind, including our perception of ourselves and our perception of other people. I will be returning to that shortly.

Overload

You can overload your mind with too much information and too many tasks to complete in a given period of time, resulting in feeling overwhelmed and then underperforming. This, in turn, can lead to exhaustion and knock your confidence and self-esteem. Subsequently, important life goals can be missed, including your relationship goals; it's clear therefore that you must not sabotage the care of your mind. For example, if you're distracted by social media all day, how much attention are you really giving your loved ones? Research on Facebook users suggests that taking a break from the site's information overload can help with stress, in the short-term at least. [25] And also, when you're so overwhelmed with tasks that you neglect the things that boost your self-esteem, such as physical exercise or learning a new skill, then how are you going to feel both about yourself and about being around other people? People notice when you're lacking self-esteem, though what they'll often sense is just a feeling of awkwardness or low energy, which they may not identify as poor self-esteem. As we saw with Gerrard, this can often result in repelling people instead of attracting them. Use your time, energy and focus wisely, because as we've seen, your choices determine what you can achieve in your relationships and life.

If you're wasting your free time and sapping your energy by overloading yourself with unnecessary tasks, your relationships will eventually suffer as a result, as will your self-esteem and life goals. Imagine how much quality time you could be spending with the significant people in your life, how much you could be helping those in your circle who need your time and attention.

By tuning in to your body, and your overriding thoughts, you can tell how overwhelmed, fatigued or fragile you feel. Use your body and your thoughts as a self-assessment tool at any given moment in order to gauge when you need to focus on self-care. For example, notice if your body feels heavy, exhausted or delicate, and if you find yourself thinking statements like: 'I just can't think clearly, my brain is so tired'; 'I'm not feeling motivated and yet I definitely want to achieve this goal'; 'I cannot bear the thought of having to make conversation with people if I go out'; 'I feel weepy for no reason'; 'I just want some time out from everyone and everything'.

⊱ OVER TO YOU ⊰

Reduce Information and Task Overload

The first thing to ensure is that the amount of information you absorb feels enjoyable and manageable. Whether the aim is to maintain happiness and health in general, or to fix relationship problems that are being caused partially or wholly by overload, it's important to manage your information consumption and task load well.

It's as simple as this: if it helps your happiness, health, relationships and self-esteem, do it. If it hinders your happiness, health, relationships and self-esteem, don't do it.

What does that mean practically? Get serious about how you spend your limited and precious time. If there are some things you know you waste too much time and mental energy on, or if you know you take on more tasks than you can handle, set some goals for how you'll change things. Remember also that sometimes sensory information overload can stem from things in your environment that you may not even consider to be contributory factors, such as music playing in the background, a flickering light, a buzzing electrical sound or a large open window downstairs that makes you feel constantly on guard for your safety when strangers walk by outside. These things can be overwhelming and cause fatigue without us even realising.

Things to consider:

- hours spent watching TV;

- having the TV or music on in the background;

- buzzing sounds from electrical goods such as a TV, lamp or refrigerator; open or unlocked windows and doors or open curtains at night;

- turning to social media, emails and internet every free minute you have;

- notifications going off on your phone or laptop;

- saying 'yes' to too many tasks;

- always helping others when your mind or body are screaming for a rest.

Set some specific written goals now, for example:

- I will spend, at most, one hour a day on social media, at the weekends only.

- I will reduce how much time I spend on activities that provide little value but cost a lot of time, energy and focus, and that hinder my well-being or relationships, during or afterwards.

Me-time

Self-care ought to be part of your daily routine, as it's a must-have rather than a nice-to-have. Particularly important to incorporate into your daily diary is 'me-time', whether you schedule in half an hour, an hour, two hours or more. However, it is also important to make it flexible. If you can only commit to less time than scheduled one day, that's fine as a one-off; and if another day you feel you need more than your scheduled dose, then take more. 'Take' is an important word here. You have to take that for yourself or others will take it from you for themselves.

Ever found yourself feeling unnecessarily angry with your spouse, overly irritated by day-to-day life or distracted from your work? You can probably thank a lack of me-time (or time-out) for that. Sometimes it's the only solution you need; other times it is part of the solution. I have met clients and workshop attendees who look like they are on the edge, or who have struggled to pursue important goals, and their eyes have lit up when I have highlighted that some me-time will help. Those eyes have sometimes lit up because the idea resonated, but other times their eyes sparkled with hope and happiness because they desperately needed someone to give them permission to do what was right when they were worried it might be viewed as selfish, lazy or wasteful. From this day on, never again must you fool yourself into believing that me-time as and when you need it is anything other than **smart, selfless, mental-health saving and goal-serving**. You cannot be happy and healthy within, or form happy and healthy relationships with others, without some time out from the world and its demands, while you recharge and replenish your energy and resilience.

⊨ OVER TO YOU ⊨

Have Me-Time

Make a habit of spending time alone every day to rest and have a mini-recharge. An hour is ideal, but even just half an hour can be so helpful.

If needs be, carve out a specific time of day and a place for you to commit to some quality me-time, so that life and your loved ones don't get in the way of this all-important routine. You may have to contract this time-out with your partner (so that they understand why, when and how long you need some distraction-free time to yourself, and help you to honour it) and find a place of sanctuary away from the family and all their daily hustle and bustle.

If others want your time or you want to give your time to others, you need to recharge and reinforce your self-esteem and resilience by frequently having some time to yourself. It can be important to let your loved ones know that you need this in order to be more loving and attentive with them and to achieve your shared goals.

⊨⊨

Andrea came to see me because she felt that she had lost her motivation and was panicking that she wasn't achieving her goals. An otherwise hard-working woman who had done well in her career, she was now finding herself 'being lazy' and 'unfocused' and she felt incredibly frustrated by it. Beginning to doubt her professional decisions, she was starting to panic. What's more, this was now having an impact on her romantic relationship, as she felt her live-in boyfriend was sapping too much of her energy and that perhaps he was becoming a drain on her energy reserves because she was not getting the time she needed to herself. She became irritated by his behaviours around the home, yet because she was feeling fatigued and foggy-headed, she was unable to communicate well with him about such issues. During our conversation, we realised that she wasn't taking time out for self-care, and she definitely wasn't getting the me-time she needed and craved, because she wasn't giving herself the permission for it. She decided to take control by taking at least an hour every day of uninterrupted me-time, and this one change alone helped her to become motivated with her work goals again, much less irritated by her partner and more proactive (Happy Relationships Pillar 3) about communicating well with him (Happy Relationships Rule #4) about what she wanted and needed in terms of cohabiting more harmoniously.

Sleep

Sleep is your recharge button, your reset button and your upgrade button all in one. Sometimes all you need is a good night's sleep. Seriously.

Sleep is your recharge button because it helps you to replenish your energy with rest and temporary downtime. Such a recharge also enables you to communicate effectively with your loved ones, because, as I'm sure you've noticed, when we are sleep-deprived we can struggle with our facial expressions, resulting in poorer communication and misunderstandings that can lead to relationship conflicts. [26]

Sleep is also your reset button because it allows your brain to process upsetting experiences, helping you to better regulate your emotions, so that you feel better when you wake the following day (i.e. calmer and less worried). Just one night of sleep-deprivation, on the other hand, can impair the function of the amygdala, which results in a continuing negative reaction to a stressful situation the next day (e.g. an ongoing worry). [27, 28]

Sleep is also your upgrade button because the brain seems able to consolidate memories [29] and problem-solve [30] while sleeping, thus helping you awaken each day with new thoughts about yourself and those around you, and the solutions you have been searching for.

And given that sleep disorders are linked to poor mental health [31] and mood disorders, such as anxiety and depression, [32] and that getting a good night's sleep can help alleviate mood and anxiety symptoms, [33] it becomes clear that we need to be proactive in ensuring that we sleep well at least most nights, if not every night. Just as we think about what we are going to eat for our next meal, we have to think about how we are going to get a good night's sleep that night.

Even if you find sleep unappealing because you would rather be living life, you wouldn't be living it with the mental health, well-being and gusto you do if it weren't for daily sleep. You cannot be as skilful in navigating your way through conversations and challenges in life if you're not getting a good night's sleep – so make it a priority!

⊱= OVER TO YOU =⊰
Get a Good Night's Sleep

A good eight hours of sleep, give or take, depending on your personal needs, is important. If you suffer from insomnia, try:

- working through your mental concerns with a solution focus, in a notepad, before you go to bed;

- not looking at emails or social media close to bedtime (for at least an hour before, preferably two);

- not having lots of light in the room when trying to fall asleep (consider an eye mask or even black-out curtains if your room isn't completely dark);

- reducing exposure to circadian-rhythm-disrupting blue light from electronic devices before bed; try not to watch a TV show or film on your phone, tablet or TV (again, at least an hour before bed, preferably two hours);

- listening to soporific music before bedtime;

- physically exercising more during the day to help tire you out and expel tension from your body, e.g. brisk walking for thirty minutes or resistance training for an hour and a half;

- having a hot shower or soak in the bath before bedtime to relax you;

- a hot foot-soak in the evening;

- a meditation exercise (like the one on page 61);

- yoga or some other relaxing activity for the last hour or so before going to sleep;

- a cup of hot milk in bed to relax you;

- avoiding stimulants like coffee or alcohol before bedtime;

- avoiding food late at night that makes you uncomfortable in bed;

- focusing the mind on positive, relaxing thoughts, like good memories;

- focusing the mind on subjects that completely distract the mind from worrying about the problems you are working to overcome, e.g. concentrate on something immersive, like a book.

Nature

Embracing nature by looking at, walking through or sitting among green spaces, flowers and trees has been shown to be very calming and anxiety-soothing, and you'll have likely experienced this yourself.

Being around nature lowers the heart rate and reduces blood pressure; it can also reduce physical pain and negative emotions, and increase positive emotions.[34, 35, 36] Looking at nature can also stop you from acting impulsively [37] – something that may well come in handy if you're in conflict with someone, for example, and considering sending a potentially regrettable text message, if you know what I mean. And it's not just being immersed in nature that helps; even just hearing the sounds of nature can calm us,[38, 39] whether you're simply listening to a recording of natural sounds, or hearing them through an open window in your home or office, or walking outside without earphones blocking the natural sounds out.

I love how nature provides us with so many ways to feel calmer, to take time out to heal and think more clearly about problems and solutions, and that it is accessible to us at all times. Regardless of whether we live in the countryside or spend most of our time in urban areas, with a bit of preparation, we can all gain access to nature in small but meaningful ways. For example, you could buy a plant for your office or home that you can look at to gain those calming, healing properties. Or you could decide upon a specific pair of comfortable walking shoes or trainers, as well as warm clothes and accessories if necessary, so that a dose of nature is always easily accessible, even if it means just going to a small green space near your office or home, or on the way home. Simply prepare your home, place of work and your life so that you can get a dose of nature, almost immediately, as and when you need it. That way, very little thinking is required to get a quick fix to either ease anxiety, tension or stress, or to calm you down for increased inner peace. It will also help you to think more clearly and problem-solve (see the following section on exercise, page 55).

Feeling hurt by what your partner has said and need some space to calm down before you say or do something you'll regret? Listen to the sounds of nature or look at nature, either from the comfort of your own home or by going outdoors. When you come back to the conversation, you'll likely have a different perspective, you'll communicate better now that you can think more clearly, you'll focus more easily on solutions, forgiveness and compassion, and hopefully you will both benefit in some way from the conversation you've had.

Feeling upset at work after a meeting or want to walk in feeling calm before a meeting starts? Get a dose of nature if you can, to ensure that you don't let a small portion of the day ruin your productivity for the rest of it and that you bring your most astute self to the meeting, ready to resolve any challenges that may come your way (e.g. defending your level of progress on a project or explaining recent decisions you've made).

Want to work out whether he is the right partner for you? Go for a walk as you think about all you know of your relationship and your own needs, wants and self-worth. In this more relaxed state, you will have the time, space and clarity of thought to really think about the relationship from all angles, and you may find that multiple walks in nature help you to finally come to the right decision.

Need to recharge your mind and body to be ready and resilient for new challenges ahead? Immerse yourself in nature until you feel that internal shift in your mind and body which tells you that you are feeling more relaxed and happy and maybe even more optimistic. Sometimes we just need some rest and relaxation to take on the world again. Without recharging ourselves as and when required, our mental faculties slow down and we lose physical energy, all of which stops us from working to our fullest potential.

Interestingly, greater happiness levels are also linked to better daylight exposure at work and at home [40, 41]. So, get more daylight, and stock up in the summer so you feel less glum when the days get darker for longer in the winter.

Clearly, nature is very helpful in regulating our emotions from negative back to positive. And here are some more activities that will help you to do so.

Exercise

There is something magical about physical movement and exercise. A well-exercised body is much more like a well-oiled machine than one that is kept dormant. Exercise affects your physical and mental health and your ability to think and problem-solve well. Let's take a look.

On a day-to-day level, exercise can help soothe stress, anger and anxiety, thus helping to take you out of fight-or-flight mode, allowing you to communicate better, solve problems more easily and make good decisions. Here's why. Stress and negative emotions can trigger the fight-or-flight response. This brain–body reaction causes near-instantaneous physiological changes that help us to fight a threat or flee from it. For example, the heart beats faster to push blood to our muscles for strength, extra oxygen is sent to our brain to increase alertness and our airways widen and we breathe faster to draw in more oxygen. At the same time, the thinking, problem-solving and decision-making part of our brain (the prefrontal cortex, located at the front of our brain) also stops working at its optimum level, [42] because if we stop to think in times of immediate danger, we can get hurt or killed. As a result, we act more instinctively (rather than thoughtfully), so that we can react to things quickly just in case they are a serious threat. Have you ever overreacted in an argument, or struggled to get your point across well? You can thank your fight-or-flight response for that. When you're not able to think well, you can end up saying and doing silly things. In a genuinely dangerous situation, it can help to fight off danger with aggressive, overt displays, such as shouting or puffing your chest out, but when you're just having an argument with your partner or your mum, you probably don't really want to frighten them off! Exercise can be a great way to calm your mind and body back down so that you can feel relaxed and peaceful, and able to bring your best self to your relationships.

But exercise can also bring long-term improvements to your mental health. Moderate-intensity aerobic exercise for thirty to forty-five minutes, three to five times a week, has been shown to be effective for treating major depressive disorder [43, 44] – potentially as effective as antidepressants. [45, 46] That's incredible and incredibly insightful! Aerobic exercise that gets your heart rate up is seriously good for your mental health.

Moderate-intensity aerobic exercise has also been linked to the production of a brain protein called brain-derived neurotropic factor (BDNF), [47] and the brain needs this protein to rewire itself when we learn new skills and create new habits.[48] So if you need to change your communication style or your conflict style, or you need to learn how to react to stressful situations or manage your anger better, you need this brain protein to help you change your bad relationship habits into good relationship habits. Moderate-intensity cardio exercise will help you do this, so integrate activities that you enjoy, which will give you a healthy dose of this each week, whether that is brisk walking, jogging or dancing.

Strength training can also be good for self-esteem, [49] soothing anxiety symptoms [50] and overall physical fitness. Yoga also seems to be effective for building resilience to stress, enhancing well-being and reducing anxiety and depression levels, [51] as well as boosting self-esteem. [52]

Walking has been found to help us problem-solve better, too, as we'll see in the Problem-Solve Relentlessly chapter (page 165), so you may also find that by moving your body as you do when walking – for example, when dancing – you discover helpful solutions to your problems. Movement is important. Remember the following whenever you are feeling miserable because you're mentally stuck with a problem or generally stuck in a rut:

A stagnant body creates a stagnant mind.
Movement in the body creates movement in the mind.

Get moving when you feel stressed or stuck, depressed or deflated, fatigued but struggling to mentally switch off. Remember the power of movement and how it can help when you need to change your thoughts and are searching for solutions to your problems.

Mindfulness

Mindfulness and mindfulness meditation are especially helpful if you have got yourself into a habit of thinking negative thoughts a lot of the time, or if you find yourself ruminating, worrying or self-criticising a lot. Mindfulness is when you live in the present moment rather than being caught up in your thoughts. Mindfulness meditation is when you dedicate a set amount of time to training your brain to be quiet and in the present moment. Successful mindfulness is immediately calming and can even feel euphoric when you get out of your head and into the present moment. You do this by focusing your mind on only what you are absorbing through your senses, and it's better if you do so with a sense of gratitude – for example, really appreciating the beauty of the branches of a tree, or the feeling of the breeze on your skin, the lighting in your home, every taste of the food in your mouth, and so on. Instead of focusing on thoughts that may be making you unhappy, you focus on just being, and feeling grateful for the life you are living. Even when there are things that are making you miserable, there are things you can still appreciate; it's just about which direction you're looking in.

Mindfulness meditation, on the other hand, has been shown to encourage our brain to become better at regulating our emotions. Just as you train your body every minute with the actions/movements/exercises you do or don't do, you train your brain with the thoughts and behaviours you use or don't use (see more on how to train your brain into different habits in the Communicate Well chapter, page 91).

To demonstrate how your thoughts can change the structure of your brain, one study asked meditation novices to use a basic mindfulness meditation practice for eight weeks. After that time, the participants' brains had physically changed. Compared with their own pre-meditation brain scans and participants who didn't meditate, the meditating participants had increased the amount of grey matter in the parts of their brain involved in learning, memory, emotion regulation, perspective taking, and processing information in relation to ourselves. [53]

What's more, in a previous study led by the same leading researcher, a positive correlation was discovered between a reduction in stress and a decrease in grey-matter density in the amygdala, the brain region that plays an important role in stress and anxiety. [54] Therefore, not thinking negative thoughts is good for your brain, helps build your resilience to daily stresses and helps you feel calmer overall.

Mindfulness can help your relationships with others, too. With repeated practice you can learn to respond more constructively to relationship stresses and conflicts, as well as learn to communicate much better with others by focusing on what's happening right now, rather than on what's been said or done in the past.

Plus, on the flip side, mindfulness helps us to deal with social rejection. Those who practise mindfulness are more resilient to the distress of rejection, because their brains work differently when experiencing rejection. [55] The left ventrolateral prefrontal cortex – a brain region that becomes active when the brain needs to inhibit negative emotions – is activated less in those who use mindfulness, and there is also less connectivity between the left ventrolateral prefrontal cortex and the bilateral amygdala and the dorsal anterior cingulate cortex, which play significant roles in the generation of social distress. It's as though mindfulness creates a buffer from the pain of social distress, resulting in the brain needing to do less work afterwards to cope with rejection.

⊱ OVER TO YOU ⊰

Use Mindfulness and Mindfulness Meditation

Mindfulness

This is how to approach being mindful. Instead of 'being in your head', get into the present by focusing on what you are absorbing through your five senses and simultaneously do so with gratitude.

For example, as you look up at the branches on trees, appreciate their beauty and how they bend and intertwine, their colour and their texture, how their beauty sits against the canvas of the sky, and so on. As you make a cup of coffee in your home, pay attention to where you are, how fortunate you are to have clean running water out of a tap, how much you appreciate the warmth, shelter and privacy of the place you call home, etc.

Mindfulness Meditation

If you have a tendency to worry all the time or a lot of the time, then get serious about retraining your brain with a simple mindfulness meditation exercise. You can use a mini version of this day to day, too.

The 'long meditation':

- Sit or lie somewhere warm and relaxing.

- Set an alarm for between ten and thirty minutes and close your eyes.

- Take three to seven deep breaths; inhale slowly, hold the breath for a few seconds, and exhale slowly.

- Mentally scan your body for any tense muscles and consciously relax each one.

- For the remaining time simply focus your mind on your breathing.

- Each time a thought pops into your mind, observe it without analysis or judgement and then imagine it floating away with the clouds or getting washed away in a river or via a powerful waterfall. Then, refocus on your breathing.

The 'mini meditation' is the same as the above but you don't have to lie down – you could be sitting or standing somewhere convenient, where it's safe to shut your eyes for a little while. Then, set an alarm for between one and five minutes and follow the breathing exercise above to relax into it.

These practices calm the mind and help generate inner peace as we learn how to live in the moment – not in our heads, not in the past and not thinking about something in the future, but right here in the present moment, just being.

Do the meditations as often as you can and work them into your lifestyle. If you find mini meditations effective and more achievable, do them daily as and when you can, and when you feel you need help to calm down or relax. If you need to make more drastic changes to your mental well-being, do the long meditations three to seven times a week. Remember, the more you train it, the more you will change it.

Cleanliness and Pampering

How the brain behaves is connected with how the body feels. That's why things like nature and exercise can be so very useful; they work by triggering physiological changes, which in turn influence the brain. But how we treat our body can also send a message to the brain about seemingly unrelated acts. Allow me to explain.

Cleanliness is something we have seen linked to godliness and goodness for centuries, and as humans we tend to associate clean with good and dirt with bad: 'My conscience is clean so I feel good'; 'they give off a dirty image, they're probably bad people'. Research has also demonstrated that the 'Macbeth effect' can occur: that cleaning the body cleans the mind or reinstates our moral purity again, [56] thus helping us to feel better about ourselves. In one study, recalling a moral transgression motivated people to want to clean their hands afterwards (when given the choice) and when they did, they felt absolved of their guilt.[57] Other research has shown that cleaning the face, rather than the hands, can absolve people of feelings of guilt and regret.[58] Studies have also found that performing an immoral act, such as lying, not only motivates people towards a preference for cleansing products over and above non-cleansing products when offered both; their brain scans also show that just imagining immoral behaviour made them feel literally dirty.[59] So remember that how you treat your body in terms of care and cleanliness impacts your mind and feelings of self-worth. Perhaps that's partly why a shower feels so good when you feel sad, anxious or morally bad, aside from its relaxing effects.

⊨ **OVER TO YOU** ⊨

Create a Positive Mind–Body Connection

Build a more positive self-image from this point on:

1. Keep your body and immediate environment clean and tidy
   every day. A shower can work as a wonderful 'reset button'
   for your emotions and physical tension.

2. Make yourself feel valuable by treating and pampering
   yourself as often as required. This can be once a month,
   once a week, or three times in one week if you really
   need a big burst of self-love. You could get a massage, a
   manicure, a haircut or new clothing; have a soak in the
   bath; soak your feet; paint your toenails; shave your
   stubble and so on. This stuff is especially helpful to do
   regularly if you suffer from low self-esteem and also if
   you're feeling overwhelmed, fatigued or fragile. Obviously,
   it won't solve all your problems, but it can help by
   boosting your confidence and feelings of worth, leading
   you to consciously and subconsciously make better
   decisions in your life.

3. Once or twice a year, it can be good to do a spring clean if
   you have a habit of hanging on to old, worn-out things.
   Every so often, throw out tatty clothes, shoes, accessories
   and other such possessions that you attach to your own
   body or personal environment, for these items shape our
   self-image by reinforcing either a low self-worth ('this is all
   I'm worth') or a healthy self-worth. If they're no longer

benefiting your self-image and self-esteem but could benefit someone in need, give them away to charity instead. Start right now: schedule and complete a spring clean during the next seven days. It's fun, feels good immediately afterwards and has an overall positive effect on your self-image and outlook as the weeks and months go by.

Nutrition

Nutrient-rich foods give the brain and body the necessary fuel they require for optimal functioning, so it's incredibly important to eat well. You wouldn't expect your car to run properly without fuel or electricity, water or engine oil, so make sure you give your body the water, vitamins and minerals it needs to do its job properly.

Long-term research on approximately 50,000 people in the UK found that increased fruit and vegetable consumption can enhance mental well-being, with the more fruit and vegetables consumed and the more frequently, the greater the positive effects. [60]

In other research conducted in ten different corporate workplace sites with adults of multi-ethnic backgrounds, people on a low-fat, plant-based diet reported significant improvements in symptoms of depression, anxiety, fatigue, emotional well-being and productivity in their work and personal life because of improved health, compared with those in the study who ate whatever they desired. [61]

Because of its integral role in our brain–body's stress response (via the connection between the hypothalamus, pituitary gland and adrenal gland – the co-working of which is referred to as the HPA axis), the state of your gut also impacts your mental health. [62] So if you easily and/or frequently experience anxiety or depression symptoms, it may be worth cleansing your gut frequently to flush out waste products and toxins, and ensuring that it has plenty of good bacteria in it, which you can do by eating a wide range of fruits and vegetables, pulses, nuts and whole grains and live yoghurt to feed your healthy bacteria, and avoid processed foods, which often contain ingredients that either suppress 'good' bacteria or increase 'bad' bacteria.

Vitamin D deficiency has been linked to irritable bowel syndrome, [63] and given that we want a healthy gut for the aforementioned reasons, *and* that vitamin D is also linked to better mental health, including positive effects on depression, seasonal affective disorder, other mood disorders [64] and physical health, ensuring you get enough is incredibly important.

Also, remember to stay hydrated. Drink plenty of water – aim for three litres a day and you'll notice how it can instantly lift your mood, slow down a racing heart, give you more energy, make you more alert and make you look healthier, brighter and younger! Sometimes those fine lines are due purely to dehydration.

Take care of your water and nutrient intake and it will help you to build a resilient, happy, healthy mind and body.

Happiness-boosting Activities

If you do the things that make you happy, you feel happy. Obvious, isn't it? And yet so often it's overlooked, perhaps because we sometimes feel guilty for doing things that are pleasurable, as if it means we are not striving to fulfil our potential. The reality, however, is that happiness helps us to be more resilient and helps us to perform well in life. So don't feel guilty for having fun. Know that you need to be happy in order to have happy relationships and a happy life. And if you do still feel guilty or selfish for making yourself happy, remember that when you are happy, you are contributing something positive to the world, making it a better place for all of us.

There are four happiness-inducing activities that have been found to be particularly helpful and easily accessible.[65] They are:

◊ **social activities**, such as spending time with friends and family;

◊ **recreational activities**, such as hobbies or interests;

◊ **achievement-oriented behaviours**, such as working on a goal that will create a sense of achievement;

◊ **spiritual activities**, such as praying, meditating and worshipping.

Happiness, combined with a belief that you're in control of your life, also results in greater health-protective behaviours, meaning that we proactively look after our health more by eating healthily, exercising frequently, not smoking and drinking moderately.[66]

Importantly, the happier we are before a challenge hits, the more resilient we will be when we face that challenge.[67] Therefore, by boosting your well-being as and when required and taking steps to maintain your happiness levels overall, the better equipped you will be to deal with any relationship challenges you face, however unexpected. It's better to always be ready for the lows, because they will come, sometimes seemingly out of nowhere; that's life. And you'll be glad you were mentally prepared when the moment comes.

⊨ OVER TO YOU ⊨

Use Happiness-building Activities to Boost Your Self-Worth and Resilience

When you maintain habits that help you to feel happy, confident and resilient day to day, it's much easier for you to resolve your relationship problems quickly, as you apply Happy Relationships Pillars 1, 2 and 3 (be happy and healthy within, be authentic, be proactive).

Schedule the following into your diary, using these frequencies to guide you:

a. **Socialise** one to two times a week. See family/friends at home, go for a meal with your partner, go out on the town, attend a meet-up or interest group.

b. **Indulge interests or hobbies** two to seven times a week. This might include arts and crafts, computer games, hiking, dancing, reading or playing a musical instrument.

c. **Be spiritual** weekly or daily. Pray, meditate, attend places of worship, read religious books.

d. **Strive for and achieve goals** daily or near daily. This could include learning a new skill, creating something valuable out of a hobby (like an album or a career), earning a university degree, getting married, creating a pension or investing money.

Also, think positive thoughts about being in control of your life.

⊨⊨

SUMMARY

When you look after yourself, you will feel happy and healthy within, compassionate, empathic, present, energetic and so on, enabling you to have great relationships with others. So never feel guilty for doing the things that recharge you, replenish your resilience, boost your self-worth and self-esteem or enhance your well-being. Reduce information and task overload, take some me-time, sleep well, immerse yourself in nature, use exercise and mindfulness, maintain cleanliness, pamper yourself when needed, eat well, socialise with loved ones, indulge your interests, work towards your goals when rested and use spiritual activities such as meditation or prayer.

Rule #3: Be a Friend

'Too often we underestimate the power of a touch, a smile, a kind word, a listening ear, an honest compliment, or the smallest act of caring, all of which have the potential to turn a life around.'
Leo Buscaglia

People are powerful. They can change how you feel about yourself and what you believe you can do, and give you a purpose to survive and thrive. Regardless of whether you are connected for work or pleasure, and whether they're in your outer circle or inner circle, at the root of all successful human relationships is a foundation of genuine friendship. When you both make friendship the basis of your relationship, you create harmony and growth, because you are both near-constantly striving to be **compassionate**, **empowering, appreciative, respectful, trustworthy and helpful**. Even if the other person doesn't reciprocate as much, you can still live in the knowledge that you brought your best self to the relationship. That's what helps you to feel good about who you are, and if the relationship ends, it helps to know that you conducted yourself in a way that gave your relationship the best chance of thriving.

Bringing these traits to a relationship allows you to walk into it feeling calm and confident; you remain present and thus see the other person for who they are, rather than being distracted by your own thoughts and 'emotional baggage'. After all, given that other humans are integral to our well-being and survival, you want to start each new relationship by giving them and yourself a fair chance of success, whether it be in a work, social or personal context.

Should a relationship break down, you want to be able to walk away from it feeling calm and confident, with no regrets, not left with any 'what ifs', and taking away with you any lessons that have been learnt about yourself and the types of relationship you want in your future. When you have put to bed your past relationships, made sense of them as much as possible and learnt valuable lessons from them that can benefit your future happiness, then each new relationship is a wonderful opportunity for something deeply fulfilling and significantly beneficial to your health and well-being. And as soon as you realise that a relationship is deeply *unfulfilling* and significantly *damaging* to your health and well-being, then you need to (a) fix the relationship problems if possible and if both parties are willing, or (b) if there is no way of salvaging what you had, thought you had or wish you had, get out of there safely. Even then, the fact that you conducted yourself in a way that demonstrated your desire to be compassionate, empowering, appreciative, respectful, trustworthy and helpful will in itself keep you safe and resilient because you have shown the other person you have valued them and done right by them, and you know you've done your best.

Therefore, every relationship benefits from friendship and every person benefits from friendship, and even though we may not necessarily want to be actual friends with our boss or neighbour or business associate or friend's friend, we all benefit, as individuals and mankind, when we each honour the qualities we bring to our friendships. For example:

◊ Empower and respectfully help a colleague who is struggling with an exercise you find simple and easy.

◊ Appreciate the friend of a friend who makes a significant effort to get to know you, whether you really feel a spark between you or not, and trust that they have good intentions until they give you reasons to suspect otherwise.

◊ Help your neighbour who is struggling to put their bins out for collection every week because they are growing old and frail. Do it with respect and compassion, empower them to feel they are still capable and self-sufficient in many other ways by boosting their confidence with genuine feedback, and sincerely appreciate and thank them for any insightful wisdom they share with you by way of stories.

When we meet others with friendship in our heart, we envelop them and ourselves in a warmth that only human kindness can create. It shows them that they are valuable, noticed and significant – which is something we all want. And like tends to attract like, so if you are a friend to others and envelop them in that human warmth, they will likely reciprocate, and then good things happen. More specifically, though, **if you consistently seek to be compassionate, empowering, appreciative, respectful, trustworthy and helpful to the other person,** be it a partner, friend, neighbour or colleague, then:

◊ each person's self-worth is boosted, because we help others to feel valuable, and we elevate our own self-worth when we treat others well and are thus received well;

◊ arguments happen relatively infrequently, as most are prevented with the friendship traits we bring;

◊ we easily broach difficult conversations with others when we need to, because we feel we will be heard and things will be acted upon, as we'll be treated as a friend;

◊ we are quick to make things right with one another, eager to let bitterness and blame go; we are happy to take ownership of our own wrong-doings out of respect for the other person and a desire to repair things quickly;

◊ we want the other person to fulfil their potential and will help them where we can;

◊ we want to keep the spark alive, whether platonic or romantic, with experiences, fun and laughter, because we appreciate one another and feel uplifted when we connect.

When things are right we nurture the relationship, because we are being a friend. And when things are wrong and there are disagreements or arguments, it's the intention to behave as a friend that makes you find solutions to your issues, as you seemingly naturally meander back to the same path – the one you wish to walk together, happily.

These are the moments where talking smartly to ourselves can help significantly, by:

◊ keeping our focus on recognising the things that are going right;

◊ keeping our focus on doing the things that will help us stay as happy and healthy as possible;

◊ keeping our focus on the direction in which we want to travel.

Remember how we spoke earlier of the long-term study which found that the happiness of one person is connected to the happiness level of friends, friends' friends and friends' friends' friends, both online through social media, and offline, with the same applying to depressive symptoms? A thirty-year research study also found that the happiness level of each spouse rises and falls together, [68] while another study found that closer friendships are linked to sharper memory as we age. [69]

Therefore, our happiness and mental health are connected with the happiness and mental health of others, which then places four responsibilities on us:

◊ First, we must take care to ensure we are happy and heathy overall (Happy Relationships Pillar 1), as how we feel will impact our loved ones and other people they know.

◊ Second, we should help our loved ones to be happy for their own sake as well as for ours.

◊ Third, we need to proactively (Happy Relationships Pillar 3) prune away negative, damaging relationships, whether in our inner circle of close friends and family or in our outer circle of less close friends and family and colleagues and associates and neighbours and other community members, or at the very least distance ourselves from them as much as possible.

◊ Fourth, we need to authentically and proactively (Happy Relationships Pillars 2 and 3) build and nurture positive relationships in our inner circle and outer circle, as our health and well-being will massively benefit.

As each human being radiates happiness to others around them, who in turn radiate it to others around them and so on, in a ripple effect, we cannot deny the power of people, the power of just one human being to affect another human being. Please don't ever be slapdash about who you let into your life, online or offline, and ensure they are, for the most part, **clearly and consistently showing you** that they are wholeheartedly compassionate, empowering, appreciative, respectful, trustworthy and helpful in the good times and the bad.

So how do we experience someone being compassionate, empowering, appreciative, respectful, trustworthy and helpful? Whether you're lacking in any of these qualities or feel someone else is in their relationship with you, here is how we experience each of these traits and why happy relationships require them.

Compassionate

Compassion can be defined as a strong feeling of sympathy and sadness for the suffering or bad luck of others and a wish to help them.

When we are compassionate with others, we are able to look beyond our own needs and emotions, such as pain, frustration and anger, as we focus instead on being sympathetic and supportive. We become less 'me-focused' and more 'other-focused', but not at the detriment of being happy and healthy ourselves. **Remember to treat others as of equal value to you, not above, not below.** That means you honour your worth while still being compassionate, otherwise you won't be building a happy and healthy relationship.

For example, a new date makes excuses for not calling you for several weeks since they'd promised on your first date to arrange a second. They have been 'ghosting' you and you have sat around wondering what the hell happened and why they're treating you this way. Perhaps you have even been questioning your own worth as a result, or at least your ability to achieve your goal of finding someone to spend your life with. Given that we have so much technology at our fingertips, you know their excuse that they've been too busy with work commitments to even let you know that they're too busy does not truly explain their lack of contact. So, because you own your worth, you let them know this is unacceptable and walk away. You realise that if they already cannot honour Happy Relationships Rule #3: Be a Friend within the first few weeks of the relationship, then it's a clear sign you are not meant to stay connected with them.

On the other hand, if your sibling shouts at you about a conversation you had with your mother about them and they're now angry, while you may be feeling hurt and defensive, you also recognise that the reason your sibling is angry is because they are panicking about the consequences of what you have said. Although you know they are worrying over nothing, you also take a moment to step back and think, 'Given what they have been through with others recently, I understand why they are panicking.' Your focus is on sympathy and a desire to help them out of the hurt, even though you do not agree with the panic or the verbal attack on you. Your compassion results in your sibling calming down and then offering you an apology for shouting at you, and now the relationship is back on track, as you both continue to 'be a friend' to one another.

Compassion is crucial as it helps you to allow for people's failings, though not at the repeated expense of your self-worth. If you've been struggling with compassion, meditation could help. In an experiment conducted over eight weeks, those who had undertaken regular meditation practice (either mindfulness meditation or compassion meditation) were more compassionate towards a fellow human being who they saw was suffering than those who had not undertaken any meditation.[70]

Importantly, as self-compassion is a precursor of compassion for others as we cannot give to others that which we will not give to ourselves, mindfulness meditation has been found to be helpful, especially for caregivers such as mental-health professionals, who could be at risk of developing psychological problems – like stress and exhaustion – due to the emotional strain their work can cause. Those who undertook mindfulness meditation experienced increases in self-compassion and mindfulness, and declines in stress, rumination and both fleeting and long-term anxiety.[71]

So meditation can help you to be more compassionate with yourself, the people in your inner circle, the people in your outer circle and strangers. If you find yourself frequently getting angry, it may be that you need to meditate or even just practise being more mindful minute to minute, so that you can be calmer and more compassionate. Use the 'Over To You' exercise on mindfulness and mindfulness meditation on page 61. It's easier to be compassionate than angry, both immediately and in the long run. Always keep compassion in your heart – it's the most comfortable way to live and the clearest way to see. It helps you to be happier and healthier within (Happy Relationships Pillar 1) and it helps you to have positive relationships.

Empowering

We can define 'empowering' as a trait that makes a person more confident and helps them feel that they are in control of their life.

When we think and behave in an empowering way, we use words that reflect our faith in another person's abilities, and use our words to make the other person feel in control, capable and confident. We demonstrate through words and actions our desire to help the other person emotionally, practically and / or financially to achieve their goals. You'll use or hear words like, 'You are intelligent and hard-working; you always do well in anything you put your mind to', and you'll give or receive offers like, 'No matter what, we'll find a child-minding solution if you need to attend that course to further your career.' It has to be authentic, though (Happy Relationships Pillar 2), otherwise they will sense you're being fake and it won't help you to have a happy relationship.

When someone encourages you to take on challenges and reach your potential, you'll feel more optimistic and confident. On the other hand, when someone discourages you from taking on new challenges or from reaching your potential, you feel pessimistic or nervous.

Everyone benefits from someone believing in them, because it helps them to believe in themselves. When we empower another human being, even if it's just by showing that we value them and care about their achievements in life, they are able to achieve more. When we are proactive (Happy Relationships Pillar 3) in helping them to achieve more, we help them to become happy and healthy within (Happy Relationships Pillar 1). Helping those we love dearly also helps us to feel happy and healthy within, too.

Research on school students has revealed that they are less likely to drop out of school and more likely to feel positive about it and be on time when they have ongoing relationships with teachers, as noted when chronically absent students were paired with a mentor for two years as part of a programme to help build the students' attendance and engagement. [72]

Importantly, devaluing and abandoning goals for the sake of increasing relationship commitment in a newly developing romantic relationship can, over time, lead to a decrease in relationship satisfaction, particularly for women. [73]

Optimism, a necessary ingredient for empowerment, leads to satisfying and happy romantic relationships over time, partially because of the cooperative problem-solving approach that ensues when you're both being proactive [74] (Happy Relationships Pillar 3).

If you want to empower your partner to do something that *you* want them to do, on the other hand (for example, if it's good for their health, well-being and longevity), research suggests that you should be clear about your request, give them reasons for it and refrain from being dominating or too forceful. [75]

In fact, a large body of research suggests that when we and the significant people in our lives have a positive attitude towards a behaviour (for example, running to lose weight or doing an online course to further our career), we feel more motivated to do that thing and take more action as a result. [76, 77, 78] In other words, when being supported and empowered by the attitudes of significant others, we're more likely to be proactive (Happy Relationship Pillar 3). So empower the good people in your life and get your loved ones behind you – and if they're not, find out why they're not and what will help them to become more supportive and empowering.

Appreciative

Appreciation can be defined as the act of recognising or understanding that something is valuable and important.

When the appreciation is two-way, we build a foundation that encourages us and the other person to stick around; this is because we feel valued and that what we bring to the table is noticed and respected. This, in turn, makes us feel good about ourselves, the other person and the relationship we have with them, and this appreciation then motivates us to continuously honour the Three Pillars of Happy Relationships with help from the 7 Simple Rules to Create Harmony and Growth. We can appreciate the big and the small things that people do for us, the multitude of ways that people add value to our lives and when someone has honoured their commitment to us, whether it's a promised night out or wedding vows.

We all have one life. We don't know how many years we'll be alive or how much of that time we'll be healthy, and we have plenty of things to do that take up our limited twenty-four hours each day, so if we're going to take up someone's time, focus and energy, they're going to want this to be appreciated, otherwise they can save these to spend them elsewhere. Complacency is perhaps one of the biggest relationship killers – don't let it kill yours. Show people you appreciate them every single time you connect, with your words and actions. It's not about being extravagant, it's about being sincere, and it's as much about acknowledging the seemingly tiny things as it is about the big things. For example, the cup of tea and biscuits you surprise your beloved with when they're overwhelmed with work can speak volumes about your love for them. The sincere 'thank yous' might be just what they need to hear. The twinkle in your eye when they cook a meal for you can leave them feeling that the two-hour chore was in fact a pleasure. Appreciation motivates people to want to do more of the same. It spurs on reciprocity and reinforces their worth as a human being. In other words, it significantly nurtures the relationship you have with them and the relationship they have with themselves.

Daily gratitude is helpful, as it boosts connection and satisfaction for both partners in a romantic relationship – the giver and the receiver – for as much as twenty-four hours. [79] Plus, appreciation may help keep the spark alive in long-term romantic relationships, helping us to increase our feeling of well-being. [80]

Both verbal and non-verbal expressions of appreciation can help in friendships and romantic relationships, with those from individualistic cultures (such as Americans) utilising both verbal and non-verbal demonstrations, while those from more collectivist cultures (such as Asians) tend to prefer the non-verbal. [81] For example, those from a more individualist culture might express appreciation by saying or writing in an email or card, 'I appreciate what you do for me' and 'I love you', and they might offer reciprocation by saying, 'I'm here if you need anything.' They might show their concern by advising, 'I'm always saying you should take care of yourself.' Those from a more collectivist culture, on the other hand, might show their appreciation through physical affection, such as a hug, kiss or holding hands, and they might do favours for the other person, such as cooking for them or buying medicine for them when they are ill. All of these acts show appreciation; some are expressed verbally, some non-verbally, but all are powerful. People show love and appreciation in different ways, you just have to learn their way.

Research also suggests that having experienced great difficulties in the past (such as divorce or the death of a loved one) can make us more appreciative about life's small pleasures in the present, so going through hardships now may serve you well in the future as you find yourself savouring the little moments all the more. [82]

Get the most out of your relationships with your colleagues, friends, family, partner and neighbours by being appreciative, but also make sure you're being authentic (Happy Relationships Pillar 2). Don't say you appreciate them or something they did when you don't. That's worse for your relationship than staying quiet. But do look for ways to express and show sincere appreciation as often as you can – and remember that the smallest gestures often speak the loudest.

Respectful

Respect can be defined as admiration felt or shown for someone or something that you believe has good qualities or good ideas.

When we admire someone, we treat them as though they are valuable. When we treat people as though they are valuable, we reinforce their self-worth, and we essentially convey that we know their reputation and time are not to be toyed with. We convey respect through how we communicate with them, by honouring commitments we have made that put demands on their time and by listening attentively to their opinions and feelings. When your respect for someone is lacking, you're dismissive of the other person's opinions and time and effort, and that isn't going to make them want to spend time with you. It will also sabotage their ability to feel happy and healthy within (Happy Relationships Pillar 1).

Trustworthy

We can define a trustworthy person as someone who is reliable and loyal.

As we share so much of our (at times secret) inner selves and so much of our heart with our loved ones, we need to feel that people can be trusted with our personal information and to protect us from emotional pain. As we cannot watch over people and how they speak about us and treat us when we are not around, we have to be able to trust that they are honouring their commitment to be loyal to us, regardless of whether they are being watched or not.

We demonstrate our trustworthiness through words that are truthful, by being authentic with people (Happy Relationships Pillar 2) about who we are, what we want and what we need, and by allowing people the ability to verify our loyalty as and when required. When we are trustworthy, we also help others to feel happy and healthy within (Happy Relationships Pillar 1), because it boosts their self-worth.

Higher levels of trust are linked to higher levels of well-being over time, especially for older adults, while lower levels of trust are linked to the opposite. [83] Therefore, trust is crucial for our personal happiness and, indirectly, for happy relationships.

In organisations where a high level of trust is nurtured and sustained, colleagues are significantly more engaged. Behaviours such as recognition of great performance, being given greater autonomy, creating a culture of openness and care, and creating group challenges that are hard but achievable to stimulate the release of oxytocin (a chemical that is released when we are shown trust and which makes us want to cooperate with others), all help people to build trust. [84] These are principles you can apply to any relationship in your life: recognition, autonomy, openness, care and undertaking challenges together.

Oxytocin plays a significant role in human trust [85] and bonding, [86] and interestingly, when romantic partners keep secrets themselves, they trust their partner less. Talk about judging others as we are (i.e. seeing the world 'through our own eyes')! If you've ever had someone repeatedly and undeservedly accuse you of keeping secrets or being a liar, it may well be because they themselves are keeping secrets from you or lying. [87] This is also a trait of gaslighters [88] – those who use psychologically abusive tactics to control others. Frequent insincerity right through to outright incessant lying are also the traits of psychopaths. [89, 90] Similarly, people who are themselves interested in alternative partners can become angry and antagonistic when they think their partner is interested in others. [91] So when people aren't acting in a trustworthy manner, it may show itself as a lack of trust in you, or as some form of aggression. Pay attention to strange behaviour, no matter how much you love the person and think you trust them. Speak to a trusted friend or seek out professional help if you think you are in a psychologically abusive relationship. And of course, make sure you are always being sincere and trustworthy yourself.

Helpful

Help can be defined as making it possible or easier for someone to do something, by doing part of the work yourself or by providing advice, money, support, etc.

Life can be tough, and we all need help sometimes, and when you help others, you show them you care, that you want them to be happy and healthy and successful. Helping others not only shows that you value and appreciate them being a part of your life; it makes you feel good about yourself, too.

Being helpful is being proactive (Happy Relationships Pillar 3); proactive about helping others to be happy, healthy, develop personally and achieve their goals, all of which helps them to be happy and healthy within (Happy Relationships Pillar 1).

In fact, research shows that we feel happier when we give to others, even when it costs us something.[92] Giving can help reduce blood pressure[93] and make us more resilient, even when we're facing tough times ourselves.[94] So sometimes focusing on being helpful can be a great way to boost our own happiness and health.

⪢ OVER TO YOU ⪡
Be a Better Friend

Be more compassionate by seeking to understand why your friend, partner or relation are feeling or behaving as they are. Be patient, be present and, whenever possible, don't take things personally. Forgive where you can and draw a line under the past when you do.

Be more empowering by using positive words that instil faith in them and their abilities and their worth as a human being.

Be more appreciative by communicating verbally and using gestures small or large, free, cheap or expensive, to demonstrate how much you appreciate them and all that they do for you, whether it be emotional, practical or financial.

Be more respectful by honouring time commitments, asking their opinion and, where necessary, their permission, and by communicating in a way that shows you value them, their time and their thoughts.

Be more trustworthy by being transparent and honest, by doing what you say you will do, by saying what you mean and by being authentic (Happy Relationships Pillar 2).

Be more helpful with your words and actions.

Questions to ask yourself to help you, help the relationship or help you to realise that it needs to end:

1. How can I be more compassionate towards them?

2. How can I empower them more?

3. How can I convey my appreciation better?

4. How can I respect them more?

5. How can I demonstrate my trustworthiness more?

6. How can I be more helpful?

7. How can I be a friend to them?

8. How can I get them to be a friend to me?

9. What's stopping me from being a friend to them?

10. What's stopping them from being a friend to me?

11. Do I need to work on my relationship with me, my self-worth, self-esteem and confidence?

12. If I am not happy and healthy within, how can I improve my self-esteem and my overall feelings of happiness and healthiness, mental and physical?

13. Is there something they have done or not done, or said or not said, that's stopping me from being a friend to them?

14. Is there something that needs to be addressed within the relationship?

15. If something needs to be addressed within my relationship, (a) what is it? And (b) how can I individually, and we together, resolve what is not working well, however old or recent the issue(s) may be?

———

Invariably, when you are not able to be a friend to someone, it's either because you have an issue with them (e.g. they have upset you and you are harbouring ill feelings towards them that are affecting your behaviours and the relationship outcomes you are achieving), or you need to address something about how you feel within yourself, or a combination of the two. Either way, Problem-Solve Relentlessly (Happy Relationships Rule #7, page 165) and being proactive (Happy Relationships Pillar 3) will help you to resolve the issue. Always start with you, though, because everything starts with us and very often it is our relationship with ourselves that needs addressing. When working with clients, I find that the majority of relationship issues exist because Happy Relationships Pillar 1 (be happy and healthy within) is missing for one or both of the individuals. So start by looking within, and then look outwards at the other person, the other people in your life and the circumstances you find yourself in.

SUMMARY

Without a strong foundation of friendship, all relationships fail, so ensure that both parties are always striving to bring compassion, empowerment, appreciation, respect, trust and helpfulness to the table, and if they're not, work to address it. If, after that, they still aren't demonstrating these traits, it's time to move on, or at least distance yourself from them.

Rule #4: Communicate Well

'Take advantage of every opportunity to practice your communication skills so that when important occasions arise, you will have the gift, the style, the sharpness, the clarity and the emotions to affect other people.'
Jim Rohn

Use communication to own your worth and show others theirs, to repair broken bridges and show you care.

Once the foundation is laid with (a) good, helpful, goal-serving thoughts about yourself, the other person, your current situation and relationships in general, (b) love and care for your mind, body and inner self, and (c) behaving as a friend would, you need to ensure your communication is helping you and your relationships to be happy and healthy.

Tell people what you want and need, and find out the same from them. Perhaps you can sense that something isn't right, or maybe they look unhappy or unhealthy. People don't look miserable or argue for the sake of it; they look miserable or argue because something is bothering them. Care enough to find out what. And if you walk around with a long face instead of sharing your wants and needs, you're doing both of you a disservice.

With good communication we also work out someone's commitment level: how much they care for us. With bad communication we may think someone doesn't care for us, but the reality might be that we're just communicating really badly and so not getting clarity, cooperation and change. **We always convey through our verbal and non-verbal communication and our actions, what we expect and are willing to accept.**

You must ask for what you want and need, and:

◊ if they don't give it, you need to find out why;

◊ if they don't want to give it, you need to find out why;

◊ if they can't give it, you need to decide if you can be without it.

The other person should be asking the same questions of you.

Effective communication in the good and bad times can spell the difference between understanding and misunderstanding, harmony and disharmony, well-being and stress, elation and frustration, relationship connection and disconnection. Bad communication, whether negative or non-existent, over time can lead to relationship breakdown and then break-up or divorce. On the other hand, good communication over time can lead to relationship satisfaction, harmony and growth. Even when it doesn't, at least you know it's because your journey together is meant to come to an end. Not everybody is meant to be in our lives forever, and that's okay.

When you get into poor communication habits with a friend, lover, boss, parent or child, because the communication leads to disappointment and conflict, it becomes emotionally painful and so eventually you might stop communicating altogether. When clients come to me because a relationship, whether romantic or platonic, professional or personal, has led to silence, the emotional distance between the two people can be greater than if their communication is fraught with conflict. When the communication is full of conflict, as bad as it is for your health and happiness, you are at least telling the other person that you care and are trying to do something about your relationship; however, when you fall silent, it can suggest that you just don't care anymore, because you've now stopped trying to repair things.

The important thing about communication is that it signals health or a lack thereof, and when it signals the latter, you simply need to look below the surface at the undercurrents. With all communication you need to look at the underlying themes as well as the words. Just as a meal comprises ingredients, so, too, does a conversation. It's not just the flavour, it's what led to that flavour:

◊ Is it unhappiness about a recurring issue?

◊ Is it anger about a specific situation?

◊ Is it worry about the future?

◊ Is it a cry for help?

◊ What are they *really* saying or trying to say, albeit ineffectively sometimes?

Just because someone is an adult doesn't mean they are going to communicate well all the time. Just because someone is intelligent or successful doesn't mean they know how to manage their emotions well, especially when speaking with a loved one, because, let's face it, we all get lazy with our communication efforts with our nearest and dearest from time to time. Sometimes we feel angry and we blurt out any old crap, without thinking about whether we're being rude or hurtful. If you love someone, or at least care about them, you owe it to yourself and them to communicate your needs, and figure out what they are really trying to communicate to you, and the best way to do that is by being a friend – Happy Relationships Rule #3 – being compassionate, empowering, appreciative, respectful, trustworthy and helpful.

Communication Is Rich with Information

When we use our words and accompanying non-verbal communication to **convey what we like, love and appreciate** about the other person, we encourage them to repeat those behaviours, because if they feel rewarded for something they have done, they will likely repeat it once their brain comes to associate that behaviour with a positive emotion. Think about how often you highlight to them that you notice the value they add to your life, that you're not complacent about what they do for you and how they make you feel, that you empower them to believe in themselves, that you reassure them when they are down, that you boost their self-image and self-esteem. If you don't communicate these positives often enough, start doing it more now, and be sure to be authentic (Happy Relationships Pillar 2) for it to have a lasting positive effect. People won't always tell you that they need this; sometimes we have to recognise and address these missing links ourselves.

On the other hand, when we use our verbal and non-verbal communication to **let people know what we feel isn't**

working in the relationship, we show we care, that we want things to be better. Sometimes people don't communicate back in the most calm, effective way, but **it's important to always listen to the subtext as well as the words and to watch the non-verbal communication** to understand what they are really thinking, feeling and saying. See if there are any inconsistencies between what they are saying and what their posture, movements, facial expressions and colour, eyes and tone of voice are saying. Our brain subconsciously notices inconsistencies between another person's verbal and non-verbal communication, [95] so if you feel intuitively that someone isn't being honest with you, even if you can't quite yet pinpoint why, pay attention to your intuitive hunch. Smart human communication is all about being aware of the subtleties, inconsistencies and anomalies, as well as our own feelings.

Notice Inconsistencies

You can notice inconsistencies when, for example, they say they are fine but their hunched shoulders and bowing head suggest they are not, or when they say they have time but their facial expression says they don't, or when they say they love you but their eyes and awkward physical touch tell you otherwise. Equally useful for identifying inconsistencies are actions. Pay attention to people's actions; their words may be uttered simply to fool themselves. Heed the signs and use them to inform your next step. Sometimes people intentionally lie to themselves because that may be easier for them than confronting the truth. Sometimes they just don't know their own true feelings, and sometimes they are afraid to be honest with you.

Use each communication as a way of gauging the health of your relationship, and if you notice warning signs that something is not right, be authentic (Happy Relationships Pillar 2) and speak up, and be proactive (Happy Relationships Pillar 3) about resolving whatever needs resolving; remember that taking action and making progress always helps you to be happy and healthy within (Happy Relationships Pillar 1), because you are dealing with any threats to your well-being and relationships.

Notice Anomalies

You can notice anomalies when someone suddenly starts behaving very differently from how they have previously spoken or acted in a given situation. Or perhaps everyone you know is happy for you about your news, yet there is one person who you'd quite rightly expect to be happy (based on your relationship) but who seems to be silently discontented. Anomalies stand out, and they stand out for a reason. Your job is to uncover the reason, work out what it means about the state of your relationship, and then be proactive (Happy Relationships Pillar 3).

And remember, if an issue cannot be resolved and it's a deal-breaker, walk away to ensure your own future happiness and health (Happy Relationships Pillar 1). Take yourself off to have relationships with those who deserve to have you in their life.

When it comes to communicating, you must be present, as discussed; really paying attention to what you are absorbing through your senses – your eyes and ears and the sensations on your skin that come from someone's physical touch. There is a wealth of significant information in all of that, information that will help you to create and maintain a happy relationship. For example, does their eye contact suggest that they care about you or lack concern? Are they listening attentively or are they distracted or disinterested? Do they calmly touch you with the palm of their hands when trying to reassure you or do they touch you hesitantly with their fingertips? Does their posture suggest they are happy or unhappy, angry or calm? Do their facial expressions suggest they are comfortable or uncomfortable in this situation, secretly jealous or sincerely happy for you? And importantly, given what you already know about them and about your relationship to date, what do all of these cues mean about them, your relationship and the current circumstances you find yourself in? To communicate skilfully, you'll need a few other strategies in your arsenal to help you honour the Three Pillars of Happy Relationships (be happy and healthy within, be authentic, be proactive). Let's take a look at those now so you can become an excellent communicator.

Minimise Your Use of Negative Words

We saw in the Create Helpful Thoughts chapter (see page 23) how our thoughts determine the direction in which our lives go via the effect our thoughts have on our emotions, our conscious and subconscious awareness and our behaviours. That applies to other humans, too. How we speak to them influences which direction they travel in – just like the words of encouragement from a parent or teacher that stay with us, sometimes for life, or the disempowering words of a frenemy that make us doubt our worth or capabilities, or the words of disdain from a partner may make us feel unappreciated or the words of kindness from a stranger may make us feel noticed. Words are powerful, so powerful that they change how the brain works.

One of the best things you can do when talking to someone is to always choose positive words over negative words wherever possible, because it will change the outcome for the better. Research has demonstrated that negative words can put both the speaker (you) and the listener (the person you're speaking to) into a fight-or-flight state.[96] Consequently, the prefrontal cortex in both your brains – the region involved in 'executive brain functions' such as critical thinking, problem-solving and decision making – becomes unable to work at its optimum level, as the brain is now focused on survival – fighting or fleeing a 'threat'. Ever said something ridiculous or hurtful in the middle of an argument and later regretted it or realised how unnecessary or silly it was? Ever struggled to think clearly, remember all the relevant points you wanted to make and get your sentences across coherently? You can thank your fight-or-flight response for that! Even when you're not really fighting or fleeing a truly harmful attack or a genuine threat to your survival, you can enter such a primal defensive and combative state that you can end up behaving in a very extreme way until you've calmed down again. Once you have, the brain's prefrontal cortex can then function at its optimal level again, allowing you to think clearly, problem-solve well and make great decisions once more.

So **choose your words wisely**, say what you want to say using positive words wherever possible instead of negative words, because both you and the person you're speaking to will be affected by your choice of vocabulary. You want them to listen and stay, not fight or run away. You want both of you to be receptive and empathic and to explore solutions, and then decide on a course of action if appropriate, yet if you're both in fight-or-flight, you can kiss that outcome goodbye. Simply think of the opposite way to say what you want to say, so that you focus on the desire or the goal, rather than the dislike or the fear. Here are two examples:

◊ 'I hate it when you spend so much of our together time on social media', can instead be stated as, 'I love it when you put social media to one side when we're spending time together.'

◊ 'It's so annoying that you keep forgetting to help out with chores around the home', can instead be stated as, 'It's so nice and I really appreciate it when you remember to help out with chores around the home.'

Notice that you're saying the same thing, but in a way that focuses on what you want, rather than what you don't want. Easy. Effective.

Focus on Goals and Desires, Rather Than Fears and Dislikes

You have to tell each other what you want in a relationship – that's part of being happy and healthy within, being authentic and being proactive (Happy Relationships Pillar 1, 2 and 3). But how you word things matters. Words are instructions for the brain. Think about whether the words you are using are taking your relationships where you want to go. Remember what we learnt in the Create Helpful Thoughts chapter (see page 23):

thoughts steer the direction your life is travelling in. Are you planting seeds of hope or doubt in the other person's mind, of love or hate, of empowerment or disempowerment, of appreciation or complacency, of confidence or insecurity, and so on? Whatever you focus their mind on, they will be influenced to work towards, consciously and subconsciously, and the more time you spend with someone, the greater access you have to controlling their mind. This is why psychologically abusive partners can destroy a person's self-esteem and perspective so easily over time, because they can control what they think, feel and do so easily with their words. Regardless of whether you're communicating on autopilot or thoughtfully, you are still shaping their happiness, health and success with your words. For example, if you frequently tell them, 'You're going to let me down as you always do,' chances are they often will, because you have told their brain to work towards always letting you down. That's the instruction you've given them, albeit by accident.

Amelie and Adam's relationship was not what it had been since they'd had their two children. Raising children is one of the most challenging experiences a married couple can go through and it's perhaps no surprise that differences in child-rearing raise their ugly head when couples are trying to navigate the different phases of their children's development, from the young baby phase to the toddler phase to the pre-teen years to the teenage years to the emerging adulthood years. This is a time when communication about the frustrations around different child-rearing practices can become quite unhelpful, toxic even.

When Amelie and Adam came for help, Amelie felt like she was drowning in motherhood and Adam was feeling unappreciated. They were arguing a lot. They seemed to have opposing views on most incidents and they were both feeling dissatisfied. One of the main issues that kept popping up and creating a lot of animosity was the manner in which Amelie felt her husband Adam was accidentally encouraging their older child to be rude to her mum. When he would notice Amelie getting frustrated or scolding her daughter, Adam would swoop in to 'protect' the child, accidentally signalling that the mother was being unreasonable (when she felt she was trying to instil good behaviour in her child). The anger and shouting that accompanied Adam's response each time allowed resentment to build up and created an unhappy home for everyone. The things is, Adam was frustrated about other aspects of his life, so when he would hear his wife and daughter quarrelling, he was already feeling unhappy and overwhelmed and so would easily get angry. And of course, when we become angry, our communication is somewhat rubbish and sometimes becomes scary. During our second session, Amelie met me alone and this allowed us to discuss how she could focus Adam's mind on the goals instead of the dislikes she had by phrasing her sentences better. For example, she started saying things like, 'We want our children to grow up in a loving environment', and 'Please talk to me when you're feeling calm so that we can have a helpful conversation', as well as asking questions that demonstrated her awareness of his challenges and her compassion and desire to be helpful, such as, 'Is there anything I can do to help you feel more relaxed?'

Just a little tweak here and there to how Amelie was approaching her conversations with Adam halted the bad communication in its path, quite astoundingly, and created a much happier, calmer, more loving home environment.

Sometimes, just one person needs to change their communication style and it can change everything for the better. It can also result in the other person choosing their words better, and if they don't, you can tell them how much easier it is for you to hear them when they communicate compassionately and respectfully, while also focusing their words on goals and desires rather than fears and dislikes.

Be Reflective, Rather Than Reactive

Listen. Watch. Think. Then respond. Good communication is about moving forward towards a mutually beneficial goal. If you just react, you might come out with utter nonsense or be accidentally hurtful, unexpectedly damaging your relationship. And if you're not sure how to respond, take the pressure off yourself by not forcing yourself to. Equally, be patient with other people; not everyone thinks, processes and communicates at the pace you do.

So often I see clients get themselves into arguments, feel incredibly anxious in the moment and struggle to get their words out or say something that they later feel embarrassed or otherwise regretful about. Consequently, when they've repeatedly communicated badly, they can experience a knock to their self-image and self-esteem. It might be that they've forced themselves into responding when they weren't ready to. You rarely owe it to anyone to respond on the spot, whether you've opened a text message and they've received a read receipt from your phone, whether you're talking face to face or over the phone, whether you've received an email and they know you respond to emails daily or whether they've seen that you're online on social media but you haven't responded to their private message. We do need to give people the courtesy of a response out of respect and compassion, but we do not need to say 'How high?' when people say 'Jump!' Instead, if necessary, respond with a sentence or two that tells the other person that you have received the message, verbal or written, and will think about it and come back to them. For example:

◊ 'Thank you for that, let me think about it and come back to you.'

◊ 'Okay, I will let you know once I've had a chance to mull it over.'

So respond when you have time, focus and energy if a response isn't necessary immediately. If they later take issue with the fact that you have seen their message but not responded straight away, just politely let them know that you don't always respond straight away because you may not have the opportunity to, and you might even add, if true, that you want to respond thoughtfully to their messages, thereby letting them know that you value their relationship. **We have to teach people through our words and actions what we expect and what they should expect**. One way to do this is to be consistent with them, and this is easy when we are being authentic (Happy Relationships Pillar 2).

When you don't force yourself into responding immediately to people's communications if you're not ready, you'll often do a great job later, one you'll be proud of, which will boost your self-image and even your self-esteem. Of course, it's not always possible to delay your response – for example, when you're in a meeting with your boss – so in those moments you could preface your response with something like, 'If I have to respond now, then I would say …' Now you have told them that this is your immediate thought, not necessarily your long-term conclusion, and simultaneously you have planted the seed in their mind that you may need some more time to answer more thoughtfully. That way, you can leave the situation knowing that you have qualified your response, making them aware that if they want more information, they can give you more time to reflect and be thoughtful.

Importantly, though, you must respond in good time and you must take the responsibility to finish that conversation when you have requested extra time. They shouldn't have to chase you, and if they do frequently have to chase you, they will likely feel frustrated and disrespected. Plus, if the other person takes issue with the length of time you take to respond then that is something you must find a compromise on (i.e. agree on what is enough time for you and an acceptable time frame for them). Equally, this does not mean that you should ask for more time for every response; don't make a habit of always asking if you can get back to someone, this is simply a tool at your disposal for when it is absolutely necessary, because when you leave conversations hanging, you may inadvertently leave the other person fatigued from having to mentally carry around your unfinished conversations.

Be Specific with People

Tell people exactly what you want, and if necessary, how and when. Words are like instructions to the brain. Let people know what they should focus on; people are busy, and only able to focus consciously on so much at any given moment, so if you say too much, they may not commit enough attention to your message, and may pick out the bit they want to focus on, rather than the most important bit you want them to focus on. The clearer and more concise you can be, the better.

Give Them a Heads-up

Sometimes we can get frustrated when we speak to someone and they respond with solutions when we wanted an empathetic ear, or they offer sympathy when we wanted help. So let people know in advance what you want them to do. When you want them just to listen, tell them so beforehand. When you want advice, also tell them so beforehand. This will help them to listen to what you have to say from the correct perspective, whether you want them to be empathetic, sympathetic, offer solutions or offer their help.

Be Present

If you want someone's undivided attention – for example, to discuss an important, pressing family issue – let them know and ask them if they are able to provide it; if they can't, they will let you know and then you can decide to speak about the matter in hand another time if you so choose. If they say they have time to give you their full attention but you can sense they are distracted, albeit halfway through your conversation, calmly and respectfully let them know that you can sense they are unable to focus right now and then, if needs be, agree to reschedule the conversation for another time when you can both commit the attention required. If you urgently need to discuss something now, let them know that you appreciate that they are busy or have other things on their mind but that you desperately need to discuss something, if they could just give you a few moments, and then keep the conversation clear and to the point. It's surprising how easily you can get through all the important information you need to when you have limited time, because you simply cut out any unnecessary details and focus on the key points. When I have clients turn up late for a session and they only have, say, thirty or forty minutes left, we still usually manage to cover everything they wanted to explore and resolve, because the focus becomes laser sharp and so the conversation is adjusted to the time available.

Being present also means noticing what's happening right now, rather than having a greater focus on past events, arguments and mistakes, whether in this relationship or in your experience with others. It allows you to absorb what the other person is thinking, feeling and saying, verbally and non-verbally, as both types of communication also reflect what is happening internally. This is all important information that you want to capture. Be aware, also, that when we glean information about someone's emotions, it helps us to work out the thoughts they had that preceded them. Research has found that we can detect emotions really quickly just from vocal sounds – such as a groan, growl, laugh or cry – in the absence of words. It takes the brain just one-tenth of a second to begin detecting human emotions from a vocal sound – faster than they can detect them from their tone of voice – regardless of whether it was a positive or negative emotion being conveyed. [97]

So get out of your head and into the present moment whenever you are communicating with someone. That way, you also allow your brain to subconsciously capture as much information as possible from the person and environment, and this is part of the information your intuition will use to help you to know what's really going on in your relationship, and help you make the right decisions for you both.

When Alice went on dates, she would be so caught up in her own head, worrying about what her date was thinking about her, how she was coming across, whether he would call her again or not, regardless of whether she was even sure she liked him yet, that she would rarely remember afterwards what her date was like – both the experience and the person. She was 38 and panicking, and she had now opened the floodgates to let any romantic partner into her life, regardless of whether he seemed to be the right person for her or not. So she went on a lot of first dates and would spend so much of it in her mind that she'd forget to form a connection with them, fail to communicate well and completely forget to pay attention to who she was actually on a date with. It was unsurprising that she had been on so many first dates.

So we got her to (a) clarify what her ideal partner and relationship would be like, so that she would own her worth instead of allowing any old person to come into her life, and (b) got her to practise being present (or mindful) during her dates. As a result, she went on fewer dates, as she had stopped wasting time going on dates with people who weren't right for her. This boosted her well-being enormously. She also went on fewer 'bad' dates, because she was being more selective and more present during dates, making her more fun to be with and making the

date more fun for her; this also boosted her self-esteem.
Consequently, she eventually started dating a man who made her
happy, and someone she had growing feelings for.

You have to own your worth before anyone else will and you
have to own your worth to be happy and healthy within
(Happy Relationships Pillar 1) and you have to be present in
your relationships so that you know who is worthy of your
time and effort.

Show Them Due Respect

Give other people credit for being intelligent enough to
understand or have an awareness of what you're discussing.
Show them respect, don't patronise them, however smart you
think you are or however unaware of the topic being discussed
you think they are. By showing them respect, they will
appreciate it and listen better, because instead of feeling
patronised or insulted and thus inclined to become defensive in
a fight-or-flight state, they'll be more inclined to hear what you
have to say, seek to understand and help where possible.

And when you're in the wrong, own it. It shows the other
person respect and earns you their respect. This can mean
apologising for what you said or how you said it or how you
behaved, and this might simply mean saying, 'Though I still
stand by what I said, I should have said it more respectfully.'

Ask More Questions, Make Fewer Statements

Get in the habit of asking questions rather than making
statements, however much you think you know it all. Statements

in a conflict situation can suggest we have made up our mind and are not interested in a dialogue, yet asking questions shows respect and a desire to understand and help where required. Also, even if you have accurately assessed the situation, by asking questions, you are asking the other person to volunteer their insights; this will lead to better outcomes.

For example, if you tell your teenage child, 'You're struggling to focus on your homework because you went to bed late all week and are lacking sleep', they may become defensive and give you other reasons for their lack of concentration. On the other hand, if you instead ask, 'Why do you think you're struggling to focus on your homework?' they may well admit that it's because of their late nights, and then you can help them with solutions for getting a good night's sleep (see Love and Look After Yourself, page 41). Even if you ask and they don't say the reason is about their late nights, once you've asked them, you've already given them credit for being mature enough to think of reasons; you've shown you care in a gentler way and then they are more likely be receptive when you say, 'I wonder whether it's because of your late nights, what do you think?' Again, you've shared your thoughts in a gentle way, and you've asked a question at the end, demonstrating your respect for their maturity.

Even very young children love being spoken to as mature people and they love having a reason for why they're being asked to do things. Whenever possible, whether with the young or old, explain why you are saying or suggesting something. By using the word 'because', people are receptive: you are explaining instead of simply telling.

Don't Assume

Allow for grey areas instead of assuming you know it all. Maybe you think the picture is black and white, but maybe it's just that you can't see the grey. Don't be so closed-minded or arrogant to think that you have evaluated a situation and absolutely know it all! You may be missing something, the grey bit in between that you haven't thought of, or couldn't possibly know about, and sometimes the grey is where the peace of mind is.

For example, perhaps you think your child is ignoring you, and you decide it must be because they don't respect you anymore. You might believe that if they did respect you, they would roll their eyes less, come down for dinner on time, tell you where they're going and speak in a more pleasant fashion. But this assumption could easily end up creating an unnecessary distance between you. It will spur you on to a course of action that is purely geared towards resolving the issue as you see it: their lack of respect for you. Meanwhile, the real issue may go unnoticed and be left to fester. What if that issue is that they are being bullied at college or that they are harbouring ill feeling over a conversation you had that they misunderstood? Find out from them and from others what the issue is and be ready to accept that you may have missed the grey when you saw only the black and white of the situation – at least then you know which issue you need to resolve. You always have to be proactive (Happy Relationships Pillar 3) in order to have happy relationships, and later, you'll learn more about how you can implement Happy Relationships Rule #7: Problem-Solve Relentlessly (see page 165) so that you can actively address and iron out any issues.

Remember, the Three Pillars of Happy Relationships require all parties to be happy and healthy within, authentic and proactive, so be sure to communicate in ways that allow for all three. Don't stifle and don't be aggressive; encourage and be calm instead. If we want to instil calm we need to communicate in a calm way. If we want to instil compassion we need to communicate with compassion. Like attracts like; you get back what you give out.

Calm Down

Now I know you may be thinking, 'But it's so hard to think clearly when I'm angry or devastated, so how am I supposed to communicate in a calm, clear, concise and compassionate way?' and you're right. That's why it's good to have some emotion-regulation strategies at your disposal. Regulating your emotions from negative back to positive is a fantastic life skill that can help you to maintain resilience, well-being and good mental health, as well as problem-solve your relationship problems diligently, to overcome them quickly. Speaking of quickly, don't let people fool you into thinking that relationship problems take a long time to fix; they don't need to, as long as you heed the warning signs and get proactive (Happy Relationships Pillar 3), and you both want the relationship to succeed. What follows are a number of effective techniques to calm your body and mind when you need to:

Breathe more slowly. When your heart is racing, because you are anxious or angry, you can proactively slow your breathing down in order to slow your heart rate, and once your heart rate has slowed to a calm pace, your brain calms down, too, allowing you to once again think clearly, communicate well, problem-solve and make great decisions.

⊨ OVER TO YOU ⊨

Use a Quick Breathing Technique to Achieve a Calm State

You can do this discreetly, anywhere, without others even realising what you are doing.

When you feel yourself getting tense, you can calm yourself by repeating these steps about four to seven times (or about a minute), eyes open or closed:

a. Inhale deeply for about three to five seconds as you simultaneously focus your mind on your heart area and imagine yourself inhaling calm into it. [98]

b. Hold your breath for about three to five seconds.

c. Exhale deeply for about three to five seconds as you simultaneously focus your mind on your heart area and imagine yourself exhaling tension from the heart.

Instead of imagining breathing in calm and breathing out tension, you might find it helpful to focus on feeling the love or appreciation you have for someone or something.

⊨⊨⊨

Go for a brisk walk. As discussed before, both the physical distance and the act of brisk walking helps you to calm down, soothe anxiety symptoms and problem-solve – sometimes all you need in order to do that is to gain perspective.

Listen to soothing sounds. Slow-tempo classical music has been shown to reduce anxiety[99] and relaxing music prior to a stressful event results in faster autonomic recovery afterwards, compared to not listening to any music.[100] The autonomic nervous system is centrally implicated in the fight-or-flight response and is responsible for regulating bodily functions, mostly without conscious thought, such as your heart rate, digestion, breathing rate and the dilation of your pupils. In other words, music helps your body to calm down faster. In fact, various lines of research looking at the effects of music on anxiety in healthy individuals revealed that listening to music can affect our blood pressure, cortisol level and heart rate.[101] Therefore, steady tempo music can help us to feel calmer by calming down the body's stress response through physiological changes.

Dance it off. Whether in your bedroom, at a dance studio or out clubbing, dancing can enhance your self-esteem and coping strategies by helping you to feel happy, even euphoric; feel released; feel energetic; feel self-confident; feel more focused; express emotions; release negative thoughts, feelings and problems; feel positive; relax the mind and feel in harmony with yourself.[102] Dancing is a great way to release tension and gain clarity, and you can feel the shift take place as you seemingly fling those negative emotions from your body. You may also find yourself problem-solving your relationship issues as you do. This will make more sense when you read the chapter on problem-solving (see page 165) and look at the power of movement in problem-solving.

Speak to someone else. Some people can boost our clarity and resilience, because they help us to feel happy, valued, loved, empowered, calm, understood, respected and appreciated. They also help us to think differently and gain perspective, and can buffer us from emotional and even physical pain. [103] Sometimes you just need to pick up the phone or have a quick text chat or meet up in person to feel so much happier and clearer and in control of your life. Negative relationships can make you question so much about your own worth and about how your mind is working, particularly if you are in a relationship with someone who is psychologically abusive, who gaslights you or manipulates you in other ways. In those moments you need the good people in your life to help you clean the windscreen, get out of the ditch you're in and drive forward towards your happiness again. Other times, you just need to calm down and be fair with the person you've been arguing with, because sometimes you're in the wrong but you'll only realise it after you have calmed down.

Do some art. If you are the creative sort, do some form of art. You will find it soothes anxiety symptoms [104, 105] and may even help you to problem-solve your relationship challenges. [106] Always remember, just because something is playful and feels like fun does not mean that it is a waste of time or that you're being an irresponsible adult just because you've got children, a partner or a boss demanding your attention. You have to get yourself back to happy and healthy before you can be a great parent, partner, employee, boss, neighbour, family member or friend, and you'll work way faster once you're feeling calm, energetic and focused, too. So do the things that feel like fun; you have to!

Write things down. By jotting down your thoughts, feelings and what you want to say to someone, you can help your brain relax and gain clarity, resulting in a much better conversation when you do speak to your friend, partner or whomever. Your brain is able to relax because by capturing your thoughts, feelings and desired communication on a notepad, physical or digital, your brain no longer needs to worry about forgetting important information. Plus, if you capture what you want to say in the form of a 'letter' addressed to the person in question (though you needn't give them the letter; in fact, it's better if you plan not to, so that you can express within it your unfiltered thoughts and feelings), you can later execute that conversation much more effectively in order to reach your desired outcome.

Plan and Rehearse

If you are nervous about a major conversation that needs to take place, perhaps because it has historically been a difficult topic to broach or because you want to ensure a positive outcome, then planning and rehearsing for that conversation is a great way to achieve your conversation and relationship goals.

The way to do this is to think about it like a sales pitch; in a sales pitch the goal is to get the sale, the pitch is planned and rehearsed, and care is taken to use words that will prevent, or at least overcome, any objections that might come your way. So:

◊ decide what you want the outcome to be;

◊ then plan what you want to say and how you want to say it, taking care to forestall any objections that might come your way, or figuring out how you'll address them if you cannot prevent them;

◊ then rehearse it;

◊ then deliver it, calmly, confidently, compassionately.

Anything important is worth planning and preparing for. If the conversation is super-important, take care in advance to ensure you execute it in the right way – for example, if you need to break up with someone in a delicate and compassionate way, or you want your spouse to defend you to your meddling mother-in-law, or you want to rebuild a relationship with ageing parents but need to change how they speak to you, or you want a pay rise from your boss but know that you'll get only one chance and about three minutes to put your case forward. Here's an example of how you might do this:

The desired outcome: Get him to stand up for me to his parents so that I can have a better relationship with them, and they with me.

What I'm going to say, including the objections I'm going to pre-empt: Babe, I need you to stand up to your parents more on my behalf so that they are not putting extreme expectations on me, which only drives a distance between us. You know I love and respect them and want to spend time with them. I know you're not used to going against their rule, so you don't feel comfortable doing so, but just a simple line or two to explain that I don't want to go to their society functions with them every week, maybe just once a month instead, would mean I could be happier, experience less anxiety and have a better relationship with them and we can all enjoy our family gatherings much more. Will you help me with this, please? I know it might feel tough, but I know you can do it and I would appreciate it so much.

⊨ OVER TO YOU ⊨

Use Effective Communication Habits

Notice Inconsistencies

If something they've said doesn't feel quite right, if you don't quite believe all is as they say, pay attention and give your conscious mind time to tell you why you felt that way.

Notice Anomalies

A sudden change in someone's usual behaviour is an alert. Seek to uncover the reason for the change.

Minimise Your Use of Negative Words

Choose positive words over negative words wherever possible, to enable a productive conversation where it will be easier to solve and resolve any relationship issues you're facing.

Focus on Goals and Desire, Rather Than Fears and Dislikes

Use words and sentences that focus your conscious and subconscious mind, and theirs, in the direction you want to go in.

Be Reflective, Rather Than Reactive

Good communication is about moving forward towards a mutually beneficial goal, so make sure your communication is thoughtful and helps you and the other person, rather than being thoughtless and hindering you both. If you need to, ask for more time to think and respond, when you absolutely require it. For example, 'Thank you for that, can I think about it and come back to you?' Then make sure you do so in a timely manner.

Be Specific with People

Clearly tell the other person exactly what you want, and if necessary, how and when.

Give Them a Heads-up

Help yourself and the other person by letting them know whether you want them to be empathetic, sympathetic, to offer solutions or offer their help.

Be Present

Instead of focusing on past events or something else, really listen and watch so that you know what they are truly saying, verbally and non-verbally, with their actions. Some of this captured information will only become relevant after time has lapsed.

Show Them Due Respect

Respect them, don't patronise them, and give sincere apologies when you make mistakes, thereby showing them you value them.

Ask More Questions, Make Fewer Statements

Ask questions rather than making statements, wherever possible. This leads to greater understanding and easier, quicker behaviour change.

Don't Assume

Allow for grey areas instead of assuming you know it all. You may have missed or overlooked important information. This way you ensure you're working with the facts, aren't misunderstanding each other, and are moving towards solutions that will work.

Calm Down

For calmer, more compassionate communication, first get into a calm and compassionate 'head space' and 'heart space'. This can mean having time-out, regulating your emotions and taking time to reflect on what's happened and what your end goal is.

Plan and Rehearse

Plan and prepare for important conversations and then deliver your message calmly, confidently and compassionately.

Rewiring Your Brain for Better Communication Habits

Practice makes perfect, they say, and while we are infallible human beings and none of us is perfect, we must be the best we can be in each relationship we have. If you think about what I like to call 'people power' – the power of one human being to affect another in transformative and life-changing ways – bearing in mind that research highlights how positive and negative relationships impact our happiness, health and longevity, and that how we handle conflict impacts our relationships [107] and our own cardiovascular health [108] and health in general, [109] you will find that we can train ourselves into better communication habits for everyone's sake: yours, theirs and mankind's.

We learn skills and form habits through repetition. Once a habit is formed, the brain tends to carry it out automatically, because it is so used to executing that habit that it starts to do so without really waiting for you to approve it. This is done in a bid to conserve energy. Maybe the habit served you once but no longer does, and maybe you created that habit on purpose or by accident. Either way, because your brain executes these habits without really consulting the conscious part of you, they can become hypnotising! So, over time, we need to check in with our habits to see if they are helping or hindering us and whether we want to keep them or lose them. When things aren't going right in your relationships, ask yourself:

◊ which habits are serving my self-image and self-esteem?

◊ which habits are sabotaging my self-image and self-esteem?

◊ which habits are serving our relationship?

◊ which habits are sabotaging our relationship?

Considering we now know that we're not at the mercy of our current habits, you can rewire, or retrain, your brain to create different habits, habits that will serve you and your relationships rather than sabotage them. Think of it like building muscle in the gym with strength training; just as you can train your body into better performance, you can train your brain into performing better, too.

Change Your Habits Easily

Changing habits is so easy when you realise what you need to do and notice just how quickly changes begin to take place. You'll notice old, unhelpful habits dissipating quickly, often without the level of discomfort you'd expected to feel. You'll notice new, helpful habits forming quickly, often surprising you and making you feel proud of how well you've adapted to a new way of thinking or behaving. I've seen clients give up daily drinking habits, change their eating habits, go from inactive to frequently active, go from always being angry and shouting during arguments to always communicating calmly and respectfully during arguments, and so on. So first, let's look at how the brain works and then how you can retrain it to lose any unhelpful habit and form any helpful habit.

The brain contains individual neurons that process and transmit information through electrical and chemical signals. To accomplish even the simplest tasks, such as walking and brushing your teeth, the brain requires a large number of interconnected neurons to work together as a team to process and transmit all the necessary information.

Now, a change of habit (breaking the old habit and replacing it with a new one) requires us to make a conscious choice to change our existing neural networks by training the brain to modify them and create new ones.

There are three useful terms from the world of neuroplasticity research that you should mentally carry around with you to help you to think about how you are rewiring your brain all the time. They are: 'neurons that fire together wire together', 'neurons that fire apart wire apart' and the 'use it or lose it' brain. [110]

In simple terms, when two things repeatedly and consistently occur simultaneously or near simultaneously, the brain begins to associate one with the other. Consequently, the occurrence of one can then trigger the occurrence of the other without much thought, if any, because 'neurons that fire together wire together'. If you then want to break a habit, you must stop indulging it, forcing the neurons to consistently fire at different times and thereby breaking the brain's association of one with the other, because 'neurons that fire apart wire apart'. The brain comes to treat them as separate 'events' rather than intertwined 'events', so that eventually one will no longer trigger the other as the brain will no longer expect them to occur simultaneously or near simultaneously.

The third term, the 'use it or lose it' brain, refers to how the brain 'prunes away' any neural connections that are not being used. This is why it's so important to repeatedly use skills we have honed so we don't lose them through lack of use. This is also partially why the brain declines in old age – we allow skills to degenerate through lack of use as the brain responds to how we are exercising it. Therefore, we can lose an old skill through lack of use, because we either 'use it or lose it', and in the exact same way we can lose (eliminate) self-sabotaging habits to the point where we have no desire to repeat them.

⤐ OVER TO YOU ⤐
Rewire Your Brain for Good Habits

Training the brain to change a habit requires a simple three-step process:

- Identify the trigger that sparks the habitual response before the habitual response is indulged, e.g. the kids running amok at bedtime (**trigger**).

- Consciously and consistently abandon the old response every time the trigger occurs, e.g. feeling bewildered and out of control and shouting at the kids (**habitual undesirable response**).

- Consciously and consistently use the new response you want to reinforce every time the trigger occurs, e.g. remembering you're in control and talking to the kids in a calm, assertive manner (**new, desirable response you want to make habitual**).

You may find it helpful to create three columns like this so that you clearly know which habits you want to abandon and lose and which you want to create and use:

What are the triggers? (e.g. things that trigger my bad habits)	What thoughts and behaviours do I currently respond to those triggers with?	What thoughts and behaviours would I rather respond to those triggers with?

Indulge in a consistent pattern for about two to three hours a day and the brain can start to make visible changes within just forty-eight hours. [III]

Changing habits is easy when you realise **you just need a period of sustained effort** when you are consciously changing how you're responding to a trigger or otherwise altering a pattern you've been following. This is just like learning to drive a car or play a musical instrument. At first, we have to consciously think about every action, but eventually we can execute the task without much thought, fairly automatically. Instead of learning how to drive or play a musical instrument, you're simply learning how to change your response to certain triggers until you do so without much thought ... fairly automatically. Just like learning how to drive a car or play an instrument, the more you practise a new habit each day, at every opportunity, the quicker you will master that habit. That habit could be, for example:

◊ talking calmly instead of shouting angrily during disagreements;

◊ asking people to do things instead of telling them;

◊ going for a brisk walk when you come home from work instead of watching TV;

◊ being present instead of scrolling through social media in the company of loved ones;

◊ having an hour of me-time each night instead of responding to work emails at home;

◊ only drinking socially at weekends instead of every night of the week;

◊ meeting up in person with a different friend every fortnight instead of only communicating online.

You must also **be as consistent as possible**, because we have a 'use it or lose it' brain. You must teach your brain to lose the old, unhelpful relationship-sabotaging habits and instead hone the new habits that help you and your relationships be as you want them to be.

Hone your communication skills and change the behaviours that need to change, whether they are communication habits, self-care habits, intimacy habits or whatever. Remember also that if you truly think a problem lies with another person, you can change your behaviour to trigger a change in their response. If you keep acting in the same way, they'll keep acting in the same way, but if you choose to communicate or behave differently, it will force them to think about how they are responding, rather than just doing so out of habit. Plus, by changing any behaviours they ask you to change that you think are reasonable requests, you essentially take away any excuses they may be hiding behind that stop them from changing their behaviours. Remove their excuses by improving upon your communication skills and bad habits, and then you can more easily persuade them to look at their own and do the same. But remember to empower them with compassion and respect – don't patronise or belittle. Affirm to yourself, 'I bring out the best in them and the best in us', and let your behaviours follow suit.

SUMMARY

Helpful communication allows you to express your appreciation, respect and compassion for another, talk about what's bothering you, forgive where possible and create positive change. Remember that people communicate in different ways, so look at the undercurrents, not just the surface value, to get a clear picture of what's really being said. If an argument or other problem keeps cropping up in your life, it's because you haven't learnt the lesson it's trying to teach you. Be authentic and proactive (Happy Relationships Pillars 2 and 3): don't suppress your concerns; communicate about them in healthy ways. Change your communication habits if you need to, and change any other habits hindering you, too.

Rule #5: Nurture the Good, Prune the Bad

Know your worth so you know when to say, 'Yes', and when to say, 'Thank you, but no thank you.'

Positive relationships are a lifeline so you need to nurture them – and they deserve to be nurtured. You have to be proactive (Happy Relationships Pillar 3). Just because the person is a member of your family or your spouse or you've been friends for years doesn't mean you can place them on hold. Sure, we get distracted with our busy lives from time to time and the ones who really value their relationship with us will be accommodating, but relationships that are abandoned for a long time can struggle to regain that feeling of connection. The more frequently we connect with people, the closer and more bonded we feel. Yes, we all have friends or family members with whom we don't connect with for ages yet we feel like we can just pick things up where we left off, but as a general rule, especially with romantic relationships and those less close relationships in our outer circle, we have to nurture our connections frequently. Even those friendships that can be picked up where we left off still benefit from regular ongoing nurturing. Importantly, when the relationship itself hits challenges, it then has a foundation of connectedness that helps buffer us from the tough times our relationship may face. Without that nurtured, happy, healthy foundation, the relationship can snap instead of bending, and things feel harder, more miserable, more hopeless than they would otherwise.

Connect Emotionally

For a relationship to form and survive, we have to connect on an emotional level. Emotional intimacy helps us to bond in both friendships and romantic relationships, and both male and female partners in romantic, long-term relationships experience higher sexual desire when they have higher emotional intimacy between them. [112]

When we disclose personal information about ourselves to someone, we feel closer to that person, whether we're in a friendship with them (same sex or opposite sex) or a romantic relationship (passionate or companionate). [113] This can be because we have a deeper understanding of one another and because we have made ourselves vulnerable by sharing information that could be used against us in some way, even if just as a judgement of us. When we make ourselves vulnerable before someone and still feel relaxed or calm within, we feel closer to that person because we feel safe after entrusting them with our vulnerability; and when we make ourselves vulnerable and feel tense or anxious within, we feel unsafe and unwilling to share more.

By discussing our inner thoughts and emotions, whether they be worries or goals, experiences or disappointments, needs or wisdom, we are showing people who we are. When they reciprocate, we discover who they are. And that's how we learn if they truly listen to us, want to get to know us, care about us, help us, trust us, find us attractive mentally or physically, and so on. There is so much **knowledge to be gleaned about the state of our relationship** via the exchange of verbal and non-verbal communication that takes place when we connect emotionally. We can see if we are distant or close, and we can see if we are getting closer or getting more distant over time. Once you know (a) where you are on that continuum and (b) where you want to travel to on that continuum, you can identify what needs tweaking in the relationship to get it to where you want to go.

Over time you realise that you either want to get closer to someone or distance yourself from them or cut them out of your life altogether. An easy way to remember this is **nurture, pause or prune**. Ask yourself, 'Do I want to nurture, pause or prune this relationship?' Some people we cannot cut out of our lives altogether, which is why we might pause/distance them – for example, a sibling we have a very unhealthy relationship with, one that frequently hurts us emotionally.

One of the easiest and quickest ways to know the correct answer for your happiness and health is to use your body as a gauge, as we discussed earlier. Ask yourself a question as you think about a particular person and simultaneously pay attention to the sensations within your body. Relationships we can and should nurture create bodily feelings of relaxation within, while relationships we can and should pause or prune create bodily feelings of tension within. Put simply, people who are good for us make us 'feel good', emotionally and physically, most of the time; people who are bad for us make us 'feel bad', emotionally and physically, most of the time.

To gauge whether you need to nurture, pause or prune a relationship, ask yourself questions like:

◊ Does my body tell me that I can trust them or that I feel unsafe around them?

◊ Does my body tell me that they reinforce a healthy sense of self-worth and elevate my self-esteem, or weaken my self-worth and lower my self-esteem?

◊ Does my body tell me that I feel more optimistic around them or more pessimistic?

◊ Does my body tell me that they mostly listen well and empathise sincerely or that they barely listen properly and either don't empathise or do so insincerely?

◊ Does my body tell me that they care when I'm discussing problems going on in my life or does it tell me that they are disinterested in my problems and therefore my well-being?

◊ Does my body tell me that they help me to feel empowered or disempowered?

When you connect emotionally, you do so to bond and learn – and if you don't bond, make sure you still learn. You want to learn from every relationship, good and bad, past and present, so that you can apply those lessons to your other relationships, present and future. As you go through life you should be getting better at relationships. Better at intimacy, better at being your authentic self, and quicker at knowing which relationships you need to nurture, pause or prune. The older you get, the more you should notice the bad relationships disappear from your life and the good relationships draw closer. When you honour the Three Pillars of Happy Relationships – be happy and healthy within, be authentic and be proactive – you actively ensure that the right people are attracted to you and the wrong people are repelled. Get the centre right with the Three Pillars, and everything else will naturally fall into place over time.

And if you want to bond with someone but feel like you have nothing interesting to say, ask them questions about their life and watch the conversation flow, or perhaps you need to be doing more with your own life so that you feel like you have something new to say. I once had a client, Brian, who thought he was boring, but he was actually bored and didn't have much to talk about because he wasn't doing much with his time other than working. Within the space of a few weeks, he had changed his habits to incorporate more new activities into his life, which meant that he had many more conversations he was able to explore. He was energised by the changes and his mental health improved, too. Maybe you also just need to change up your lifestyle a bit, if you feel as Brian did. You could do more socially so that you have more experiences to learn from and talk about (adventures with friends or activity / meet-up groups), you could research some interesting topics on the Internet, take a course in something you always wanted to learn, or read some interesting books, for instance.

Also, remember to be present. Put your phone away, and if you can't help yourself from becoming distracted by it, switch off the volume and place it face down. The world will manage without you, but your relationship may not survive if you pay more attention to your emails, social media and calls than the person you're meant to be connecting with right here, right now. Phone usage, including social media usage, has been found to cause conflict in romantic relationships, and even have an indirect impact on depression, relationship satisfaction, life satisfaction, infidelity and divorce. [114, 115]

Zena and Richard were losing the romantic and friendship connection between them because he complained that she was always on social media when he came home from work, which was usually late. Zena complained that Richard was always on his work emails as soon as he got home, but Richard said he was always on his work emails because she was always on her phone. What are we doing? We need to connect with the people who are in the room with us. Phone and social-media use should be reserved for when you're alone and you have nobody nearby to connect with, bar the occasional email you have to urgently respond to or the odd social media post you may need to publish for the sake of your business ... and even then you can use software to automate it if it's a major bone of contention in your relationship. Think about what you're saying to someone about their worth when you sit with them and are more interested in your phone and the other people you can access through it, rather than connecting emotionally and/or physically with them. If you think that doesn't insult their worth, think again. And they may not say anything to you about it – heck, they may not even consciously realise how it impacts their self-esteem and well-being straight away, but over time, it most probably will, and then, when it erupts as an argument, you may think they are making a big deal over nothing. But it's not nothing, it's what you're saying about their value and how much you appreciate them being a part of your life and spending their limited precious hours with you.

Connect Physically, Romantically and Non-Romantically

Human eye contact and human touch are incredibly powerful, intoxicating even. That's the power of human-to-human connection. People power. We know that lonely people die earlier than well-connected people, so connecting not only buffers us from life's negatives, it is intimately linked with our survival.

When we touch someone romantically or non-romantically, physiological changes occur. For example, massage decreases cortisol and increases serotonin and dopamine. [116]

Cortisol is a hormone released during stressful situations; serotonin is a neurotransmitter that helps regulate your mood and helps you feel happy; dopamine is a neurotransmitter that rewards us when we learn, helps movement and creates feelings of euphoria, bliss, motivation and concentration. Stress is at the root of many illnesses, mental and physical, and therefore touching people is one way that we can help one another to prevent illness and live more healthily.

Oxytocin, a hormone released during human touch and sex, at least partially influences emotions, including happiness, attraction, love and affection. [117] Oxytocin also plays a significant role in the regulation of bonding behaviour between romantic partners. [118, 119] It increases positive behaviours – such as agreeableness, positive regard for the self and partner, consolation and increased eye contact – in response to negative behaviour during conflict between romantic partners, and also reduces cortisol levels, [120] which suggests that when this is the case, individuals in conflict can experience less stress. Therefore, physical touch isn't just useful in the good times, it can also help you during the bad times, like when you're in the middle of a difficult conversation. A loving hand on the back, a gentle squeeze of the upper arm, holding their hands in yours mid-conversation, can help calm them and the situation and make you more compassionate.

Even specific emotions are communicated via human touch, including anger, fear, disgust, love, gratitude, sympathy, sadness and happiness.[121] This is because different types of touch convey different emotions. For example, anger is associated with pushing and shaking; love is associated with hugging and stroking; sadness is associated with nuzzling and hugging; and sympathy is associated with hugging and rubbing. Furthermore, the duration and intensity of the contact differs for the different emotions. For example, anger is predominantly conveyed through strong and moderate touch of shorter duration, while sadness is characterised by predominantly light touch of moderate duration. Interestingly, women have been found to be better than men at accurately decoding the meaning of someone's touch.[122]

Eye contact, on the other hand, facilitates communication and helps us to express intimacy as well as social control.[123] Eye contact allows us to infer whether someone is paying attention to us or to someone or something else – even children as young as two days old prefer to look at those making eye contact with them.[124] We're more likely to act in a cooperative way if we feel someone is watching us,[125, 126] and we're also more likely to believe someone's statements if they are looking directly into our eyes as they speak, compared to when someone averts their gaze as they speak.[127] Interestingly, we're also inclined to trust people with dilated pupils and to withhold trust from people with constricted pupils, [128] and we intuitively use pupil dilation to help us make decisions about who we can trust in social situations. [129] And yes, we do naturally infer what people's emotions and social intentions are based on their eyes, and focus more on them than on any other facial features in order to read a person's complex mental state. [130] How innately wired for reading non-verbal communication we are. So use eye contact to learn what other people are thinking and feeling, to demonstrate interest and to build intimacy and trust.

The best thing to do is trust your intuition because we humans are wired to identify non-verbal communication; trust the feeling you get and trust the answers that instantly pop into your mind as you think to yourself, 'What is this person's non-verbal communication conveying about how they feel in general, or about me, or about this situation?' Your conscious mind may only later deliver the answers to you, but in the immediate moment, just trust your mind and body's subconscious awareness of what the other person is saying about their relationship with you and their intentions.

Additionally, sexual intimacy is incredibly important for romantic couples. Given that one's partner is usually the only person who can satisfy one's sexual needs, each individual in a romantic relationship owes it to their partner to offer sexual intimacy of a mutually beneficial frequency and quality. Attempts at physical intimacy among married and cohabiting couples results in more relationship satisfaction, better couple communication and less couple conflict. [131]

And the research is very telling when it comes to the power of human connection. When couples pursue 'approach' relationship goals, focused on things like **fun, growth and**

development, they have a greater sexual desire for one another on a daily basis. Such 'approach' relationship goals also help buffer them from any decline in sexual desire over time; they have greater desire on days with positive relationship events and experience less of a decrease in desire on days with negative relationship events, compared with individuals who focus less on fun, growth and development. [132]

Importantly, a long-term study on married couples in mid-life found that those who are sexually satisfied in their relationship tend to be satisfied and happy within their marriage, and that marital quality in turn helps with marital stability. [133] Sexual intimacy also has both an immediate and long-term effect as sex helps marital partners to feel bonded as they experience an immediate 'sexual afterglow' for up to forty-eight hours, and those who reported stronger lingering feelings of sexual satisfaction reported higher levels of marital satisfaction both at the beginning of the study and four or six months later. [134]

So if you're in a romantic relationship, make sure your sexual intimacy is fulfilling for both of you. Thanks to social media, online gaming and so on, the lure of infidelity is more easily accessible than ever,[135] and it's becoming increasingly difficult to keep a romantic relationship for life – and sexual intimacy is an integral part of that.

Also, don't ever use social media, online gaming, chatrooms, meet-up groups or legal or illegal drugs to distract you from your relationship problems. If you do, you're not being authentic or proactive (Happy Relationships Pillars 2 and 3) and you'll therefore let the problems continue and usually worsen. No amount of distraction from real problems will resolve or dissipate them. You have to fix them yourself, and you should use the seven simple relationship rules to help you. If you notice that you are distracting yourself from your relationship problems, know that this is a red flag telling you that something in your relationship requires your immediate attention.

Have Fun

It's important to share experiences to build memories together. Unsurprisingly, good memories are vital for our future happiness; we feel happy when we recall good memories, and when people ask us how we feel about a certain relationship, our brain is forced to trawl through the associations we have with that person. When we recall more good memories than bad, recall mostly fun and exciting times rather than boredom or pain, we feel positive about the relationship, the other person and, importantly, where our life is going. After all, as we age and become aware that we have lived more years than we have left, we want to feel that we have spent our time well, whatever that means for each of us. In that same vein, what fun means is specific to each individual too. This is another reason why we must be authentic (Happy Relationships Pillar 2), because then we know which people we want to spend our time with–the ones who match our personality and motivations, or complement them, as opposed to those who don't. Authenticity is powerful. It tells people who you are, and it tells you who you are.

Be clear about how you want to spend your time. Being aware of the values you like to live your life by helps you to make these great decisions. For example, here are just a few values to consider – you may think of others to add to the list – which may be important to you and that you would rather the people in your inner circle shared, too:

◊ Love, Flourishing, Freedom, Intimacy, Security, Adventure, Power, Passion, Comfort, Health, Integrity, Accountability, Honesty, Candour, Dependability, Commitment, Determination, Ambition, Fairness, Faithfulness, Generosity, Compassion.

When you need to bond more with those close to you, activities that force you to work together as a team are helpful, as they strengthen your sense of friendship (Happy Relationships Rule #3). Remember also that corporate research has shown that team challenges help build trust and make you more engaged.

Research has also found that when long-term romantic couples engage in self-expanding, new activities together that they haven't experienced before, they increase their sexual desire for one another and their sexual satisfaction. They also experience general relationship satisfaction, which is sustained over time.[136]

Keep things fun, keep growing, and you will help the relationship stay exciting – and it doesn't have to be sky-diving or bungee jumping if that doesn't float your boat, it just needs to be something that is exciting and new for you both.

Aron hated the fact that when he came home from work, all Rachel wanted to do was watch TV, even though she was complaining about the fact that she never got to see him. This made him stay at work late on some evenings, because he felt it was pointless going home to such an unsatisfactory evening, especially as he was working hard and craved some fun in his downtime. Eventually, Aron told Rachel how much it was bothering him and how it made him not want to spend time with her, and so she became proactive (Happy Relationships Pillar 3) and started to organise various fun activities for them to enjoy together every week, or at least every other week. This boosted their relationship satisfaction, and their sexual intimacy.

Have Shared Goals

Life can get distracting. We can forget about what's really important – our health and our relationships – when we are so busy pursuing our personal goals. If all your relationships disappeared, would you enjoy your life achievements so much if you had no one to share them with? Would you rather be poor and have a strong inner circle of loved ones or would you rather be rich and utterly lonely, with nobody to care about and nobody to care about you? And here's a tough question: would you rather be ill and surrounded by loved ones or healthy and completely alone? Doesn't that latter question highlight how central to our happiness and survival our relationships are?

Self-care, self-love and giving ongoing attention to our relationships are necessary for happy relationships (and to be happy within yourself – Happy Relationships Pillar 1), so think about how often you reinforce them. A good way to ensure that each of these acts remains a central feature in your life is to schedule in a specific time for them. Every minute spent is a minute you're never going to get back, so when you repeatedly squander that time, your brain tends to realise that something feels unsatisfactory in your life, whether it is how you spend time alone or how you spend time with your loved ones.

It's always after some time spent indulging a boring routine that a spouse says, 'All we ever do is ...'

And when you see your friends you might find yourself saying, 'Shall we do/go somewhere different this time to mix things up?'

And when you see your siblings you say, 'You know, we haven't done ___ for ages!'

That evaluation and calculation is going on in your subconscious mind. Plus, when you are so focused on your personal goals or woes that you become completely distracted by them, shared goals help to keep your focus on the life you share with your significant others. Otherwise you tend to nurture them less than you should, and sometimes that chasm becomes too big to cross. Then, suddenly, your lives are completely separate and either one or both parties begins to feel that no bridge can reconnect them. So **think about how you can grow together, rather than apart**. It can be simple, small goals, from dining in a restaurant you've never eaten in before or going on a nature walk every other weekend, to bigger goals, such as going hot-air ballooning, leasing a new car, buying a holiday home and anything in between – whatever keeps your focus on your life together, so that as you meander off achieving your own goals, you still come back to 'us' every so often. This reminds the subconscious brain that you are connected, however distracting life can become.

Research suggests that one possible reason for lower relationship satisfaction, commitment and overall life satisfaction is making fewer planned tangible investments together, which then has an impact on the well-being of the relationship and the individuals concerned. [137] Planned tangible investments help to keep your focus on your life together and they can be things like having shared possessions, getting a joint bank account, and making a joint financial investment with one's partner.

Given that we are social creatures who have one life to live and limited time to live it, it is perhaps unsurprising that finding meaning in life as couples age together also results in better perceived relationship quality.[138] Again, this affirms what we have been talking about: that we need to be happy and healthy within (Happy Relationships Pillar 1) in order to have happy relationships.

Always remember that both parts of the relationship unit have to be happy for the relationship to be happy, so aim to find something that appeals to you both. Also remember to compromise when necessary, though, by finding a happy medium. If one person likes thrill-seeking sports and the other is afraid of them, perhaps you can still share the experience with one of you cheering the other on from the sidelines. Then you can reciprocate with something the other person is more fond of. Likewise, perhaps one of you has a profession or hobby that the other person can become involved in somehow – for example, helping your partner to learn lines for a play and cheering them on when they perform.

Play to Your Strengths

Instead of being frustrated by your friend, family member or partner for their inability to do something well, be a team and play to your strengths. Relationships are central to our survival. In fact, at our core, our motivation in life comes down to our desire to survive. We earn a living to survive, we address our mental and physical health concerns to survive, and our relationships help us to survive. So whatever the relationship you are in, being a team helps you to survive and thrive as an individual and as a partnership.

There is no point in being antagonistic, dismissive or disempowering with someone just because they are not good at something that you deem important, because then you are sabotaging yourself by not trying your best to make the relationship successful. Help the other person to become better in the areas of life that they are lacking, and by doing so you will help them and indirectly help yourself, too.

In relationships, people bicker about the other's lack of X or apparent refusal to do Y or seeming inability to be responsible for Z. This can lead to frustration and a questioning of the relationship. However, sometimes your partner isn't doing something because it isn't a strength of theirs, and what they and the relationship need is a better strategy, not just a load of animosity. For example, maybe your partner just isn't good at managing money. For the sake of your happiness and the relationship's success, you need to approach the problem with a team mentality. This could mean that you play to your strengths by taking more responsibility over the finances to begin with. Over time you could be proactive (Happy Relationships Pillar 3) by helping them to become better at managing money, but until that point, you could decide to take ownership over that role so as to avoid repeated arguments, relationship problems and relationship dissatisfaction. Once you've helped them to improve that area of their life, they will feel happier about themselves, you'll feel happy about their growth and you'll have a more harmonious relationship as a result. Relationships are about recognising that we all have different personalities and skills. The important thing is knowing that we have to play to our strengths, rather than getting frustrated by each other's weaknesses, which in the long term will only be to everyone's benefit.

Communicating on an Unseen and Unheard Level

We hear a lot about verbal and non-verbal communication, but there is another form or communication that takes place, which is neither seen nor heard. We communicate with others on an energetic level, too. This simply means that our body communicates with other people's bodies by falling into physiological synchronisation with them, allowing us to detect inner emotions and thus thoughts and intentions, too. Allow me to explain.

First of all, it's important to understand that the human heart has its own independent complex nervous system, known as the 'heart–brain'.[139] As a result, the heart can and does make many of its own decisions independently of the brain and is in a constant two-way dialogue with the brain. The heart beats because of an electrical signal generated from within your heart muscle.[140] The electromagnetic field produced by the human heart can be detected up to several feet away and can actually register in the brain activity or body surfaces of people who are in close proximity to the other person or touching them, such as their legs and forearms and scalp.[141]

As different emotions create different heart-rhythm patterns, our emotional state is encoded in our heart's electromagnetic field,[142] making it possible for our heart to communicate our emotions via the electromagnetic field it emits, to other people nearby or to those we're touching. Think about how you sometimes hear people say, 'I got a weird vibe from him', or 'I feel relaxed in her presence.' Is it possible that you can pick up on people's thoughts, intentions and feelings because your body is picking up on the energy that their heart is emitting? Let's have a look.

Research suggests that when people get themselves into a calm, positive ('coherent') state, they can influence others nearby to achieve the same, as noticed by changes in the 'receiver's' HRV (heart rate variability).[143] Importantly, if the person 'sending' the calm, positive state to the 'receiver' focused on trying to change the other persons HRV, the results weren't so great, but when they merely focused on achieving that calm, positive state themselves, they were able to change the HRV of the other person as a by-product of their own internal state. Think about how someone being in a bad mood can affect the mood of everyone around them. So how is your emotional state affecting those around you? How are your emotions affecting your friends, partner, parents, colleagues and customers, the moment you walk into the room?

Your heart can also synchronise with a loved one's heart rate,[144] and respiration has been found to sync up when romantic partners are seated a few feet away from each other in a quiet, calm room, with no speech or touch taking place.[145] In both experiments, strangers' physiology did not synchronise, suggesting that our loved ones have an especially powerful ability to affect our emotions, either positively or negatively, and vice versa.

However, in an experiment with strangers playing a trust game, it was found that when we build trust with another person, our heart rates do synchronise.[146] So even with strangers, a form of communication can take place between people that isn't seen or heard. Trust seems to lead to at least one type of physiological synchronicity, which begs the question: when we feel tense or anxious around someone, is it because our heart rate is not synchronising with theirs, which causes an internal uneasiness that tells us they are a potential threat of some sort? Think about this in your own life. Sometimes you meet someone and instantly feel at ease with them, and other times you meet someone and feel uneasy around them – you can't explain it, you just sense something. Sometimes you can sense how someone is feeling by actively trying to tune in to what you think you can 'feel' coming from them on an unseen, unheard level, by how your body feels in their presence. Try it. After all, intuition research finds that our heart can detect information in our external environment and react to it, even when we're not consciously aware of it.[147, 148, 149]

When we're in the company of supportive friends, family members, colleagues, teachers or a therapist, do we suddenly feel calm and optimistic partly because they transfer their compassion to us, allowing us to think more clearly and problem-solve more easily, beyond the effect of any helpful words they've spoken? Given that bodily functions such as our heart rhythm and respiration rates can sync up with those of others, and that emotions influence our HRV, we need to think about how the people we come into contact with may be influencing our thoughts, emotions and behaviours, and how we're affecting others around us – particularly, as the research shows, those we have close relationships with.

Be a Gatekeeper of the Relationships in Your Life

Online and offline, people will make their way into your life, for better or worse, and your job is to be the best security guard you can be at the entrance to your heart and mind. In other words, be proactive (Happy Relationships Pillar 3). Who do you let in? Are they good or bad guests? How long do you let them stay? Does their residency bring value or danger into your life, and how quickly do you show them the door when they have outstayed their welcome?

Some people may enter your life via online means such as social media, online gaming and unsolicited emails, others offline through chance meetings at work, parties, the gym, the park and more. Every time someone tries to enter your life, online or offline, you should be vetting them by asking yourself questions and checking in with your bodily sensations, to help you decipher whether you want to grant them access to your heart, your mind and your life. Also remember that you can choose what sort of pass they get at the gates. Is it a day pass only, a lifetime pass or something in between? Remember that you can revoke their pass at any time; monitor their activities to know whether you want to renew their access each day or revoke it.

In this hyperconnected way that we now live, people affect our attitudes (hello, propaganda and activism), our relationships (hello, lust and infidelity), our mental health (hello, healthy and unhealthy thoughts, instructions and behaviours) and our habits (hello, empowerment and disempowerment).

Whether online or offline, we absorb messages from others consciously and subconsciously, and those messages affect us every single day whether we realise it or not.

Research is increasingly linking the use of social media to divorce, [150, 151] and family law solicitors are also noting an increase in people citing it as one of the factors leading to their divorce. [152]

We also saw earlier that human emotions are contagious, online and offline. We know that people have been the victims of 'cat-fishing', whereby someone has created a fake identity on a social-network site and has then used that fake identify to deceive a victim, whether for revenge, to gain a self-esteem kick or destroy someone else's marriage. In other words, we don't always know who we're even connecting with and what their true intentions are for us and our life.

Research also finds that some people make friends with you on Facebook for downward comparison, [153] so that they feel better about their life, and this may be the case on other social-media platforms, too. That suggests they are not going to be supportive of you when you achieve positive things in your life, and if there are people in your life who do not want the best for you, they will sabotage your self-image and self-esteem, even if it's just in subtle and subconscious ways.

Social media is also a place where the risk of infidelity is increased. [154] If, via social media or online gaming, you allow random, unvetted strangers into your life whom you've never met in person or have met only very briefly, you don't know their intentions for you or your relationships. At the extreme end, some, to boost their own self-esteem, may encourage you or your partner to have an (emotional) affair with them when you're feeling sad and confused, and you or your partner may make this choice because it's so accessible when you're feeling this way. On the other hand, some might come along and provide you or your partner with a mere distraction, which you use to suppress your true feelings about yourself or the relationship, thereby allowing any problems to fester as they remain unaddressed.

The thing about people is that you can't always be sure that they are who they say they are. They may say they support you, but make comments to sabotage your relationships or your reputation; they may say they are happy for you, but they are really behaving as though they are jealous of you, making comments that are shrouded in a 'sympathetic' statement or a back-handed compliment but are actually designed to knock your self-worth and confidence. Beware of wolves dressed in sheep's clothing. This is why staying alert for red flags, asking yourself important questions and tuning in to your bodily sensations are so important and so damn helpful. Sure, we all fall prey to liars and deceivers from time to time, but as long as we do our best not to, and provided we learn valuable lessons from those experiences and put them to good use in our future (relationships), it's okay. Life goes on. The bad times eventually fall behind us. We move forward wiser, stronger and sleeker … so long as we always stay alert at the gates to our heart and mind and so long as we keep on learning from each relationship we have.

⊨ OVER TO YOU ⊨

Nurture Positive Relationships, Prune Away Negative Ones

Only surround yourself with people who reinforce your well-being and sense of self-worth. If they frequently make you question your self-worth, proactively knock your self-esteem or otherwise threaten your well-being and your life goals, whether intentionally or not, you need to remove them from your life or minimise the time you spend under their influence.

Trust the bodily sensations you feel and the emotions they conjure when you interact with them:

- People who are good for us make us 'feel good', emotionally and physically, most of the time.

- People who are bad for us make us 'feel bad', emotionally and physically, most of the time.

Actively learn from each relationship. Tune in to the bodily sensations you experience most frequently around each person, online and offline. Trust yourself to know who is a threat to your well-being and who is a friend.

Identify the threats, improve the relationship or distance yourself from it if you can't. Remember: nurture, pause or prune. If you feel someone may be somehow sabotaging your self-esteem, relationships, happiness, health or outright safety, online or offline, ask yourself questions like:

- What is it about them that sabotages my self-esteem, relationships, happiness, health or safety?

- What do they say and do that suggests they are more of an enemy than a friend?

- What are the characteristics of relationships that truly make me feel valuable, happy, healthy and safe, and don't endanger my other significant relationships, that I don't experience with this person?

- To whom can I explain my experience who will understand and tell me if I am right in my suspicions that this person is a threat to my self-esteem, relationships, happiness, health or safety?

- What can I do to help improve this relationship, if anything?

- How can I ask/get them to start treating me with respect and compassion?

- What can I do to minimise my time spent around negative relationships?

- What can I do to maximise my time spent around positive relationships?

Sometimes, overcoming relationship problems requires changing habits in yourself and/or others, and though you can't force people to change, you can change how you behave, thus forcing them to respond differently. Retrain yourself into new habits, using the exercise on page 123 to help you.

Stock up on people power. To socialise with good people regularly, consider reconnecting with old friends or estranged family members, with the intention of starting over with a clean slate if you can. Go out and make new friends through local classes, meet-up groups, colleagues and existing friends (by attending parties, etc.). Just be around people, and only people who are good for you. Get away from bad people, or as the case sometimes is, especially in the online world, get bad people away from you and your loved ones. Remember that positive relationships are priceless for good health, happiness and longevity, so you must invest your time and effort in them. When you do, your mental and physical health will thank you. Spend time with the good people in your life when they need it as much as when you need it; give them your time, attention, respect and compassion. Be thoughtful and make sure you are there to support them in the bad times and to celebrate with them in the good times.

Vet everyone, for your health, happiness and relationships' sake. Regardless of whether you or somebody else invited a person into your personal social network, don't be afraid to cut them off just because they are already in it and/or have been in it for a while. Sometimes it takes time to vet people; simply tell yourself, 'You have now been vetted. Your application has been denied. Goodbye!' and then hit delete, physically on your social media account or mentally.

<hr />

People shape your character, your self-esteem and your life. You are valuable, so ensure that the only people allowed to

stick around are those who consistently treat you as valuable. And if they don't, you know what you need to do for your own happiness, health and longevity.

SUMMARY

People affect our well-being and our lives, so vet the people in your life continually. You can revoke their access to your life at any time, or at least limit their access if you can't block them out altogether, and by doing so you reinforce your own self-esteem and tell the world what you're worth. Just remember to nurture, pause or prune – your happiness and health depend on it.

Rule #6: Achieve Personal Goals

*'Man maintains his balance, poise and
sense of security only as he is moving forward.'*
Maxwell Maltz

When we're dissatisfied with some aspect of our life – for example, our career, our body image or a hobby we've been working hard on – it often creates a ripple effect, leading to relationship problems. I've seen clients who were unhappy in their career and consequently unhappy in general. I've seen clients who persistently took their work and work-stress home, distracting them from family time. I've seen clients who were anxious about the future of their business and career and allowed it to take a toll on their relationships and mental health and well-being. And I've seen clients sabotaging their self-care because their work–life balance is completely out of control – their life is work, work, work, with little sleep, me-time or play-time.

Then there are the people who have been fighting to lose weight, get fit and generally feel better about their body. They can be miserable at home, lack confidence in the bedroom and lack confidence in general, shying away from social activities, shunning dating and even thinking that nobody will love them as they are.

Then there are the people who have been pursuing a hobby or interest, but their achievement level to date hasn't been as they hoped it would be.

Our work life and our other desired achievements shape our daily enjoyment of life, our self-image, our self-esteem and our confidence, and, when the goal is related to our survival, such as earning an income, our feelings of inner calm as well. The older we get, the more questions such as 'Have I achieved what I thought I would have achieved by this age?' loom over our head. Now we have people forcing their success or so-called 'success' down our throats on social media, which in turn makes us look at ourselves and, whether we know it's silly or not, compare ourselves to them and even judge ourselves.

So when you feel dissatisfied with your life achievements, career, your decision to have children or not, your side projects or similar, notice how this is impacting your relationships, so that (a) you don't incorrectly blame your relationships for your current unhappiness and (b) you realise that you need to do something about it before you sabotage an important relationship for nothing, either by calling time on it for the wrong reasons, having an affair that it may not survive or saying hurtful things that cause real damage.

What I've always found in coaching is that the majority of the presenting issues in a person's relationship stem from something they need to work on in themselves – their skills, their happiness, their health. Once you have addressed what needs addressing within your own personal life, separate from anything associated with any other human being in your life, you will often have very little to address about the relationship itself. Happy, healthy relationships fall into place when you are happy and healthy within.

Don't blame your relationships for the things that make you unhappy about your own life. If you do, you'll ruin the relationships you have, which you may want to keep for the long haul, and you will go through life deflecting from the real issues, never resolving them and forever dragging them along with you into the next relationship and the one after that and the one after that, and so on. So before levelling blame at someone or something else to the detriment of your own future happiness, ask yourself what's really bothering you. In Love And Look After Yourself (page 41) we looked at self-care strategies to help you maintain good mental and physical health and boost your self-esteem. We can call that your inner world, and that inner world impacts your outer world. Now let's focus on your personal outer world, which also impacts your inner world and your relationships.

You must make sure that you are happy and healthy within (Happy Relationships Pillar 1) and proactive (Happy Relationships Pillar 3) when it comes to your relationship with yourself by achieving your personal goals, so here are some simple rules to help you.

Set Goals That Truly Motivate You

If you're not truly motivated to achieve a specific goal then, after a while, you won't put in the necessary effort, and eventually you'll give up because your brain will stop you from pursuing a goal that you don't genuinely want to achieve. Every time I come across a client who says they want to achieve goals X, Y and Z, but at the same time label themselves as a procrastinator or lazy, I always know that it actually means they have been setting themselves goals they were not truly motivated to achieve. They were never a procrastinator or lazy; they simply pursued several goals that they shouldn't have pursued for one reason or another. Consequently, they tell themselves that they are innately no good at achieving goals because of some flaw within them, but that's never the case. Never. So don't worry if this resonates with you. There is a reason you have failed and we're going to set that straight right now. No more daft goals, no more damaging your own self-image as a result.

People set goals they are not truly motivated to achieve, and then don't see them through to success for a number of reasons, for example:

◊ They felt obliged to pursue a goal based on someone else's expectations (a parent wanted them to follow a particular career; a partner expected them to take on a project; a friend said, 'Try this diet', etc.).

◊ They had not taken into account that they had grown, changed and no longer wanted to pursue that particular goal, and were only doing so based on past thoughts and desires.

◊ They had more pressing goals to tend to first. Their subconscious mind knew that this goal was not the priority to divert energy and focus to, but their conscious mind had not yet caught up with their brain's evaluation of the current situation.

Listen to your intuition. Only set goals that you are truly motivated to achieve – it's important for a healthy self-image and for your life and relationships. The time you spend pursuing the wrong goals is time you can't spend on your relationship with yourself and others. Equally, the time you spend on pursuing a relentlessly unhealthy relationship is time you can't spend pursuing and enjoying a happy, healthy relationship.

Set Realistic Goals

If you set unrealistic goals, however much they make you feel excited and confident initially, that excitement and confidence will soon give way to reduced energy levels, a lack of motivation and disappointment in yourself, because putting the effort into achieving something unachievable will eventually feel futile. You will divert that energy to other tasks and goals instead. Our time and energy is limited as it is. Your brain will stop you from pursuing an unrealistic goal because it will, again subconsciously, compute that there is no point in pursuing it, and eventually your conscious mind will catch up with it and you'll stop. Unfortunately, in the process, you can knock your confidence and hinder your self-image.

Set the Main Goal and Small Stepping-Stone Goals

To give yourself the best chance of achieving a goal, you should make it specific, like a SMART goal. SMART stands for specific, measurable, attainable, relevant and time-bound, and you are three times more likely to achieve your goal if it is SMART.[155] For example, 'I will visit a friend every other Saturday from 3 p.m.'; or 'I will go power-walking every

Monday, Wednesday and Friday between 6 p.m. and 7 p.m.'
SMART goals tell us at a glance what we are going to achieve
and when we are going to achieve it.

As is clear from decades of research, proper goal-setting is
vital if you are serious about meeting your targets. It helps us
in four distinct ways: [156]

1. Goals direct our mental attention and physical behaviours
   towards activities that will help us to achieve them and
   away from activities that are irrelevant to achieving them.
   So setting a specific goal stops us wasting our time, energy
   and focus on other pursuits, helping us to achieve our goals
   more quickly.

2. Goals that stretch us lead us to make more effort than goals
   that don't.

3. Goals affect our persistence. When given the choice, we
   will work longer on a difficult task than on an easy task. We
   will also work faster when we have tight deadlines than
   when we have loose deadlines. This again demonstrates
   that goals influence our focus and behaviour.

4. Goals affect our behaviour indirectly. Goals propel us to
   discover information and strategies that will help us to
   achieve our objectives.

I've always said to clients that they should keep their goal at
the forefront of their mind – whether through the use of
affirmations or by reviewing their goals once or twice daily –
because when we do, our conscious and subconscious minds
then spot, grasp and create opportunities to make that goal a
reality. Otherwise, opportunities can arise that you might easily

miss, and even if you do spot them, you may not take advantage of them, and you may not put in the extra effort to create opportunities to achieve your goals. Goal-setting research appears to agree, so here is an easy way to remember it:

> **'When I keep a goal at the forefront of my mind, my conscious and subconscious mind will spot, grasp and create opportunities to make this goal a reality.'**

So, set specific goals, SMART goals, and once you have done this for your ultimate end goal, repeat the process for the smaller steps you will need to take in order to achieve it, so that it feels manageable rather than overwhelming, motivating instead of demotivating. That way, you can get excited at each step of the process, as you get closer to achieving your main overarching goal. Reward yourself (in healthy ways) when you achieve the smaller 'stepping-stone goals' to help keep that motivation high. Effort followed by reward, followed by effort, followed by reward is a good way to keep moving effortlessly forward. Also, sometimes the pursuit of a goal can be challenging, so in those times it can be easier to focus on the reward you are going to give yourself than the effort it's going to require to get there.

⊱═ OVER TO YOU ═⊰
Set Realistic, Specific Goals

1. List every realistic goal you want to achieve during your 4 week plan to a happier relationship. These should be end goals and stepping-stone goals.

2. For each end goal, write down why you are truly motivated to achieve it (what will happen if you do achieve it, what might happen if you don't).

3. For every important goal that you want to achieve (end goals and stepping-stone goals), create a written SMART goal, e.g.:

   • I want us to feel close and connected again by (date/month/year).

   • Every Monday, Tuesday and Thursday we will spend quality time together at home talking intimately and connecting physically, from 6:30 p.m. till 7:30 p.m.

   • Every Wednesday we will spend from 7 p.m. till 10 p.m. doing a fun activity together, whether it's dining out, indoor rock climbing, salsa dancing, going to the cinema or some other form of fun.

   • Every Saturday and Sunday morning between 9 a.m. and 10 a.m. we'll have breakfast together as a family.

Remember, good goals tell us, at a glance, specifically what we are going to achieve and when we are going to achieve it.

Also remember – whether in your mind, on paper or in conversation – that if you're discussing goals or changes, only ever talk in terms of what you want.

———

Have a Clear Vision of What the End Goal Is

The more crystal clear your vision of your end goal, the more easily you'll work towards it, because then the satellite navigation system or 'satnav' in your mind can work out precisely what it needs to do to get you from where you are to where you want to be. To help you with this, you should write a description, and review and visualise it frequently.

When we visualise something in our mind in very minute detail, imagining what we can see, hear, feel, smell and taste (if relevant), the brain behaves as though we are actually doing that thing in real life. [157] Therefore, you can trick your brain into believing that you are practised at something that you haven't actually done before, so that when you come to do it in real life, it feels familiar and easier than it would do otherwise. You can train your brain in this way in the comfort of your own home, as you sit or lie, relaxed and safe. Set an alarm for seven or ten minutes, close your eyes and visualise away. For example, visualise yourself delivering an upcoming presentation with confidence.

Visualising our future selves also helps us regulate our emotions. [158] It can switch negative feelings such as nervousness or self-doubt into positive ones, such as calmness and confidence.

And remember to be consistent and keep going until you get there. One day off the wagon does not a habit break, so don't use one day, or even one week, of laziness or forgetfulness as a stick to beat yourself with – or as an excuse to give up.

⊨ OVER TO YOU ⊨
Boost Motivation

When motivation for a goal is dwindling, refocus your mind and re-energise yourself with excitement and self-belief. Here are some ways to do this:

Create a 'goals poster' or 'vision board' with images and words depicting your goals, taken from magazines or printed off the internet. For example, an image of the type of suit, handbag, car or house you want to own, or holiday destinations you want to visit. Place the poster or board somewhere you will see it frequently, so that you consciously and subconsciously absorb the goal reminders over and over again.

Talk positively to yourself using statements to affirm thoughts and qualities that will build motivation and self-belief.

Access motivating images that depict your goals, via your phone or computer, as a portable version of your goals poster or vision board. You can store images on your phone or tablet so that you can access them as and when you need a boost.

Visualise your future self once you have achieved your goal, in every detail.

Get uplifting support from your significant others or, if you have no such person you can ask, a professional could help, or an empowering support or meet-up group.

SUMMARY

A crucial part of being happy and healthy within, and having happy relationships with others, is about focusing on personal growth and setting yourself specific, realistic goals. Keep things clear, keep things simple and take action.

Rule #7: Problem-Solve Relentlessly

'Maybe you are searching among the
branches for what only appears in the roots.'
Rumi

When relationship problems strike you need to be authentic and proactive (Happy Relationships Pillar 2 and 3) so that you are honest with, and true to, yourself and the other person. If you are also happy and healthy within (Happy Relationships Pillar 1), then the process of problem-solving any relationship issues becomes much easier.

Think of problem-solving as using your brain like a satnav, but rather than moving from one address to another using the route identified, you're moving from the problem to the desired outcome by using the solutions identified by your brain. In a nutshell, problem-solving requires that we:

a. clearly know what the problem is (A);

b. clearly know what the goal is (B);

c. search for the answers we need to move us from A to B until we have succeeded.

That's it! From today onwards, always focus on moving yourself from A to B, from where you and your relationship is (A), to where you want it to be (B), until you've worked out the solutions and reached your goal. That's how you achieve happy relationships – by always focusing on finding and implementing solutions. If you try everything in your power to honour the Three Pillars of Happy Relationships (be happy and healthy within, be authentic, be proactive) but the relationship is still unhealthy, even toxic, you can walk away for the sake of all your other relationships, your mental health and your well-being, knowing you gave it your all. This way you can feel confident there will be no regrets following you around in later life, no 'what ifs'. And remember that you may need to use problem-solving (moving from A to B) to be happy and healthy within (Happy Relationships Pillar 1) or to begin living authentically (Happy Relationships Pillar 2) and to help you to be proactive (Happy Relationships Pillar 3).

Working out the solutions that get you from your relationship problem(s) to your desired outcome(s) ('A' to 'B') is something you will do on and off both:

◊ in your mind as you go about your day-to-day life;

◊ in your mind and on paper during a time set aside specifically for it.

So here are my favourite problem-solving, solution-finding strategies that I encourage people to do because they are super-easy, fun, effective and can work really quickly.

Asking Good Questions

First thing's first, whether you're problem-solving in your mind or on paper, you'll need to ensure you are telling your mind to search for answers – using statements won't help but asking questions will. Statements suggest to your brain that you've made your mind up and are not searching for answers. Questions tell your brain, 'Go find this answer for me.' The type of question you ask is important, too, because it determines the results your brain will come up with, just like the search terms you type into Google. So, for effective problem-solving, you must ask your brain questions that focus on solutions, rather than problems, and you'll need to tell it that you are in control.

Let's assume that Rebecca is having marital problems, with arguments a regular occurrence. Rebecca is desperate to fix her marital problems, so she starts trying to solve them with one of these two questions. The first is problem-focused and disempowering; the second is solution-focused and empowering:

◊ 'Why is it that, whatever I say, he always misunderstands me and we always end up arguing?'

◊ 'How can I communicate differently so that my husband understands what I am trying to say, and we can have a relaxed discussion about it?'

Problem-focused questions focus the mind on the problem. Solution-focused questions focus the mind on the possible solutions. Empowering questions highlight that we have responsibility over our own lives, and they nurture our well-being and make us proactive. Disempowering questions suggest that we lack control of our own lives, hindering our well-being and making us inactive.

Tune in to your bodily sensations to know if you are asking yourself a solution-focused, empowering question or a problem-focused, disempowering question. The former will make you feel lighter and more relaxed; the latter will make you feel heavier and more tense. Your mind will also tell you which one you're asking: the former will make you feel in control and optimistic; the latter will make you feel somewhat helpless and pessimistic.

Always remember, whatever we focus our mind on frequently, we work towards consciously and subconsciously, so focus it in the direction you want to go in. Always! Yes, we need to look back to learn important lessons that will help us to understand what sorts of problems we need to address within our relationships with ourselves and others. But once you've got those lessons, face forward towards your goals and desires and you'll move forward in your relationships much more quickly. If you spend too long looking in the rear-view mirror, you're going to have accidents in your life and you'll struggle to reach your destination (goals and desires) – if you reach them at all, that is. So focus your mind on good, empowering questions that will help you to be happy and healthy within (Happy Relationships Pillar 1), have positive relationships with others and recognise any that you need to prune away for your own happiness, health and survival. Remember also to ask others good, empowering questions, too, when you're searching for solutions to your relationship problems.

Brainstorming

Now you can ask yourself good, solution-focused, empowering questions as you go about problem-solving in your day-to-day life, and you can also brainstorm on paper. Brainstorming on paper is fantastic, as it allows you to start with a blank sheet. It can help to write in the middle of that blank sheet of paper, or wherever you feel comfortable, either (a) the solution-focused, empowering question you want to answer or (b) a few keywords. For example:

◊ What can I do to help raise my self-esteem easily?

◊ How can I build better relationships with my ageing parents?

◊ How can my spouse and I get the excitement back into our marriage?

Or:

◊ Raise self-esteem.

◊ Better relationship with Mum and Dad.

◊ Exciting marriage.

As you add ideas and inspiration to the page, it usually helps to form long-term memories from them, which means you don't have to worry about forgetting them; you have a written record, and can therefore conserve your energy and focus for creative problem-solving. Plus, you can then continue problem-solving easily in the forefront of your mind (consciously) and in the back of your mind (subconsciously) as you go about your daily life, because you have easy access to those thoughts. If you suddenly have ideas or epiphanies and you don't have your brainstorming paper nearby, note them in your phone's notepad – that way, you won't forget them and you can add them to your brainstorming paper later.

Get additional inspiration and help from conversations with family and friends, the internet, the library, shops, local services, professionals, and any other places or people that are happy to help.

You must capture all thoughts and ideas, regardless of how silly they may seem, without judgement, as recommended by Alex Osborn, a high-flying advertising executive who wrote an influential book in the mid-twentieth century called *Applied Imagination: Principles and Procedures of Creative Problem-solving*, [159] as you will then do your best problem-solving. You also never know which idea will come in useful later on. Sometimes the subconscious mind knows what is correct, important or needs attention, while your conscious mind needs time to catch up.

Research has actually revealed that our subconscious mind makes decisions before we consciously become aware of them and then 'consciously make' those same decisions! [160] You may write down something that seems ridiculous, but it might be because your subconscious is already aware of the importance of this information, when your conscious mind isn't.

So, let your mind freely seek out answers and solutions, keep asking good questions and make all problem-solving a work-in-progress, whether you're doing it in your mind or on paper.

Physical Movement

Have you ever felt stuck, unable to find the answers to what you're mulling over, only to suddenly realise those solutions (or at least have ideas that move you forward) the moment you get up and go for a walk?

Movement in the body somehow creates movement in the mind, allowing you to be more reflective, introspective and solution-focused and to have better conversations with people – and there's a reason for that. When you're walking, whether indoors on a treadmill or outdoors in a built-up area – not even necessarily in nature – the very act improves your 'divergent thinking', that is, your ability to use creative thinking for generating ideas. [161] What's more, the researchers also found that walking produces both an immediate and a residual effect on our creative thinking, meaning that we will generate significantly more creative ideas while walking, and afterwards once we have sat down and some time has elapsed. So jot down your thoughts and ideas during and after your walk (try not to trip up!). You'll be so glad you got that idea down if it's something that's going to save one of your significant relationships and create harmony and growth.

Another fascinating thing about these findings, though (aside from the seemingly magical power walking has over the human brain), is that even just getting up and moving around for a few moments can help you change your perspective, create greater clarity and generate new answers and epiphanies. Therefore, if you cannot (be bothered to) get out of your home, office or university to go for a walk, but you need to get out of the mental rut you're in, try moving to a different part of the room and sitting or standing in a different direction, or moving to a different part of the building altogether. You might even have a quick dance, as mentioned earlier (see page 113), if you have a little more time and energy. It might not seem like it would work, but sometimes we just need a little movement or a change of scenery to bring fresh emotions and dramatic insights.

Daydreaming

I've been mentioning how you can problem-solve your relationship challenges in your mind as you go about your day-to-day life. The great thing is, sometimes you can be daydreaming while doing some other routine task, such as cleaning, gardening, showering, and so on, and out of nowhere, your mind will deliver ideas that your subconscious has been working on while your conscious mind has been busy. You'll have noticed this when you've been focused on some task and suddenly a significant thought comes to you. In support of this, studies have found that when we daydream, we are actually using more than just our brain's 'default network' (the bit that handles easy, routine tasks); the brain's 'executive network', which handles complex problem-solving, also becomes activated. [162] It is possible that the brain is problem-solving our challenges as we daydream. To make the most of this, induce daydreaming by focusing on a simple task and then allowing your brain to wander; for example, have a shower, iron some clothes or do some gardening. The shower seems to work especially well, perhaps because it requires such little conscious thought and simultaneously relaxes the body and the mind, too, allowing the problem-solving region of your brain to work at its optimum level.

Sleep

Getting a good night's sleep helps your creative problem-solving abilities, as the brain seems able to make connections between previously unassociated information already stored while we sleep [163] and creative thinking can be hindered by just one night of sleep deprivation. [164] Even naps can help us to problem-solve better, so if your brain seems to be slowing down and you're struggling to think clearly, napping may help. [165]

⊨ OVER TO YOU ⊨
Use Problem-Solving Strategies

Every day, or at least every other day, spend five to thirty minutes (or longer) seeking solutions to your relationships challenges. The more motivated you are to resolve your relationship problems quickly, the more often you'll spend time problem-solving in your head, on paper, as you go about your day or during time specifically set aside for it. When you're highly motivated, you'll usually do a lot of this problem-solving in your head during your day-to-day life, pausing only to make notes as required.

Today and every subsequent day, use the following techniques:

- Ask yourself goal-focused, solution-focused, empowering questions that start with who, what, when, where, why and how.

- Brainstorm your answers and any other notable thoughts you have, with pen and paper. Welcome and capture all ideas with self-compassion.

- Further explore the thoughts and ideas that stand out as the best and most likely to be useful. Ask yourself further questions, or brainstorm further on new sheets of paper for each of these.

- Use physical movement to get your creative juices flowing.

- Use activities that help induce daydreaming.

- Use SMART goals (see page 157) as and when required, e.g. to help you set goals around the steps you need to take to be proactive (Happy Relationships Pillar 3) and thus resolve your relationship problems.

Treat all problem-solving as a work-in-progress and keep your brainstorming pen and paper somewhere accessible at all times so you can add to your notes as you go. Feel free to do more than thirty minutes of problem-solving at any one time.

Persistence is vital and pays off. Keep asking good questions and searching for answers, sometimes consciously, other times subconsciously, because the more time you spend thinking consciously about your goals and any challenges you need to overcome, the more time your subconscious mind will spend thinking about them.

Positive Emotions

As we need our prefrontal cortex – the problem-solving, decision-making part of the brain – to be working at its optimum level, we need to regulate our emotions from negative back to positive, even if just temporarily, so that we can come out of the fight-or-flight state and have a great problem-solving session. Use tips from the Love and Look After Yourself chapter (page 41) and the Communicate Well chapter (specifically page 97) to help you. But even if you are already calm, by purposefully inducing positive emotions, you enhance your problem-solving abilities.[166] So before you sit down to brainstorm or go for a 'creative walk', do something to put yourself in a positive mood, such as watching a motivational or funny video, talking to someone who lifts your mood, listening to music that always makes you feel positive, and so on.

Make It a Work-in-Progress

Remember to spend some time on and off, consciously problem-solving your relationship issues and then throwing them to the back of your mind to allow your subconscious to carry on problem-solving them for you while you get on with your day. Whether during the day or just before you sleep, tell your brain, 'Go find me the answer to ...' (followed by a solution-focused, empowering question). If you're going to be talking to yourself, you may as well tell your brain exactly what you want it to do. Words are instructions to the brain. Instruct it well. Be proactive. Achieve the relationships you want and rid your life of those that are stopping you from being happy and healthy within, and from having happy relationships with others, too.

SUMMARY

All relationships hit challenges and obstacles from time to time. These are learning moments and growth moments if you stop to notice them and address them. If your self-esteem matters to you, and if your relationships matter to you, the motivation to problem-solve will already be present. Then you simply need to ask yourself good questions, brainstorm notes, use movement to help you and persist until you have resolved whatever is in the way of you having a happy relationship. If, after all your problem-solving, thinking and action, you realise that it's time to say goodbye, then you can do so in the knowledge that you gave the relationship your all, leaving you with no 'what ifs' in the future. And that sort of peace of mind is priceless.

Part 3:
The Happy Relationships 4 Week Plan

4 Weeks to a Happier *Us*

'To pay attention, this is our endless and proper work.'
Mary Oliver

So remember, guys and girls, people are powerful and relationships are integral to your survival. Keep things simple, lose any bad habits that are hindering you and your relationships, and create good habits that will help you and your relationships.

Do this by always taking steps to honour the Three Pillars of Happy Relationships:

1. Be happy and healthy within

2. Be authentic

3. Be proactive

and help yourself to do so with the Seven Simple Rules to Create Harmony and Growth:

1. Create helpful thoughts

2. Love and look after yourself

3. Be a friend

4. Communicate well

5. Nurture the good, prune the bad

6. Achieve personal goals

7. Problem-solve relentlessly

Think now about which relationship habits you need to change from bad habits into good habits, whether what you say to yourself affects your self-esteem, how you manage conflict, how sincerely you demonstrate appreciation, how respectfully you communicate, how frequently you look after your mind and body, how consistently you pursue your personal goals, how you spend your time with loved ones, and so on.

To have happy relationships you need to indulge in a few simple activities every day, every two to three days or every week, so let's look at some easy, fun changes to your daily / weekly habits to help you create a happier relationship in just four weeks. Right now, take ten to thirty minutes (or more if needs be) to create your personalised 4 week plan so that you can achieve 'a happier *us*' in a relatively short space of time. Four weeks from now, you'll be surprised at how much your relationship will have changed for the better with just a few tweaks, if you commit to these tweaks wholeheartedly.

Create Your Personalised 4 Week Plan

Below, you are signposted to the detailed 'Over To You' exercises that will help you to quickly and easily achieve happier relationships and create harmony and growth over the next four weeks and beyond. **Some exercises won't be relevant to you:** if you have already achieved the goal in 'Your objective' statement, just skip to the next one in the list.

Remember that our daily habits shape our mental and physical health, our happiness, our relationships and our life, so start immediately to create and consolidate new habits that serve rather than sabotage you and your relationships, lose the old unhelpful ones, then maintain what works for the long haul. Where you are now is the result of your habits to date; where you'll be in the future depends on what you do from this point on. To help yourself stay on track, use the 'Over To You' exercises below to create your personalised 4 week plan and schedule ongoing activities into it.

Examples of SMART goals are in the 'Over To You' exercise on page 160. Below, there's an example of Week 1 of a personalised planner to help you visualise yours. In the proceeding weeks you might move things around, add goals and increase or decrease the frequency and length of activities.

	Monday	Tuesday	Wednesday
Week 1	Positive thoughts and solution-focused conversations, 24/7 Meditation, 6.15–6.45 a.m. 30 mins brisk walk, 5.30–6 p.m. Me-time, 6–7 p.m. Dinner, conversation and relaxation with spouse, 7.30–9 p.m. Problem-solving session, 9–9.30 p.m. Good sleep, 11 p.m.–7 a.m.	Positive thoughts and solution-focused conversations, 24/7 Meditation, 7.15–7.30 a.m. Problem-solving session, 12–12.30 p.m. Me-time, 6–6.30 p.m. Dinner, conversation and relaxation with spouse, 7–8 p.m. Make progress on goal X, 8–9 p.m. Good sleep, 10 p.m.–6 a.m.	Positive thoughts and solution-focused conversations, 24/7 45 mins brisk walk, 6.15–7 a.m. Me-time, 6–6.30 p.m. Hobby Y, 7–10 p.m. Good sleep, 10.30 p.m.–6.30 a.m.
Week 2			
Week 3			
Week 4			

Thursday	Friday	Saturday	Sunday
Positive thoughts and solution-focused conversations, 24/7	Positive thoughts and solution-focused conversations, 24/7	Positive thoughts and solution-focused conversations, 24/7	Positive thoughts and solution-focused conversations, 24/7
45 mins brisk walk, 6.45–7.30 a.m.	Meditation, 7.15–7.30 a.m.	Meditation, 10–10.30 a.m.	Breakfast with spouse, 9–10 a.m
Problem-solving session, 5–5.30 p.m.	30 mins brisk walk, 5.30–6 p.m.	Problem-solving session, 11.30 a.m.–12 p.m.	See extended family, 11 a.m.–2 p.m.
Dinner, conversation and relaxation with spouse, 7–8 p.m.	Me-time, 6–6.30 p.m.	Me-time, 12–4 p.m.	Me-time (incl. pampering), 3–5 p.m.
Make progress on goal X, 8–10 p.m.	Socialise with a friend, 8 p.m.+	Date night with Spouse, 8–9 p.m.	Quality time with spouse, 5–7 p.m.
Me-time, 10–11 p.m.	Good sleep, 1–9 a.m.	Good sleep, 1–8.30 a.m.	Good sleep, 10 p.m.–6 a.m.
Good sleep, 11 p.m.–6 a.m.			

Self-Assessment Leads to Self-Awareness

TUNE IN TO YOUR INTUITION

Your objective: To understand your thoughts and feelings, and make good decisions.

Dose: As and when required.

How to: Use the 'Over To You' exercise on page 15.

Happy Relationships Rule #1: Create Helpful Thoughts

UNDERSTAND THE EFFECTS THOUGHTS HAVE ON YOUR LIFE

Your objective: To be averse to sabotaging yourself with negative thoughts.

Dose: Do this on Day One of your 4 week plan.

How to: Use the 'Over To You' exercise on page 29.

CREATE A HABIT OF TALKING POSITIVELY TO YOURSELF

Your objective: To use your thoughts to steer your life in the direction of your goals and desires, including being happy and healthy and having happy relationships.

Dose: Every second of every day.

How to: Use the 'Over To You' exercise on page 35.

Happy Relationships Rule #2: Love and Look After Yourself

REDUCE INFORMATION AND TASK OVERLOAD

Your objective: To minimise overload so that you can increase your energy, focus, well-being and self-esteem.

Dose: Daily.

How to: Use the 'Over To You' exercise on page 45.

HAVE ME-TIME

Your objective: To recharge for your own mental and physical health and happiness and relate better with others.

Dose: Daily.

How to: Use the 'Over To You' exercise on page 48.

GET A GOOD NIGHT'S SLEEP

Your objective: To allow your body to perform its necessary functions for mental and physical health and well-being.

Dose: Daily.

How to: Use the 'Over To You' exercise on page 51.

USE MINDFULNESS AND MINDFULNESS MEDITATION

Your objective: To feel happier, calmer, more compassionate, and deal with stress and rejection easier.

Dose: One–five minute mini-meditations as and when required, or ten–thirty minute long meditations, three–seven times per week if required.

How to: Use the 'Over To You' exercise on page 61.

CREATE A POSITIVE MIND–BODY CONNECTION

Your objective: To elevate your self-image and self-worth and feel happier.

Dose: Maintain cleanliness daily. Pamper yourself as required.

How to: Use the 'Over To You' exercise on page 64.

USE HAPPINESS-BUILDING ACTIVITIES TO BOOST YOUR SELF-WORTH AND RESILIENCE

Your objective: To feel happier and to boost your self-worth and resilience for relationship challenges.

Dose: Socialise one or two times per week; indulge interests or hobbies two to seven times per week; be spiritual weekly, daily or as desired; strive for and achieve goals daily or near daily; think empowering thoughts daily.

How to: Use the 'Over To You' exercise on page 69.

Happy Relationships Rule #3: Be a Friend

BE A BETTER FRIEND

Your objective: To be compassionate, empowering, appreciative, respectful, trustworthy and helpful with those in your life.

Dose: Every minute you're interacting with someone.

How to: Use the 'Over To You' exercise on page 87.

Happy Relationships Rule #4: Communicate Well

USE A QUICK BREATHING TECHNIQUE TO ACHIEVE A CALM STATE

Your objective: To get yourself into a calm state on cue.

Dose: As and when required.

How to: Use the 'Over To You' exercise on page 112.

USE EFFECTIVE COMMUNICATION HABITS

Your objective: To communicate well to achieve positive
relationship outcomes.

Dose: Every minute you're interacting with someone.

How to: Use the 'Over To You' exercise on page 117.

REWIRE YOUR BRAIN FOR GOOD HABITS

Your objective: To create good habits that will help you to be
happy and have fulfilling, healthy relationships.

Dose: Daily, every opportunity you get to lose your
goal-sabotaging habits and create goal-serving habits instead.

How to: Use the 'Over To You' exercise on page 123.

Happy Relationships Rule #5: Nurture the Good, Prune the Bad

NURTURE POSITIVE RELATIONSHIPS, PRUNE AWAY NEGATIVE ONES

Your objective: To surround yourself only with relationships
that nourish your self-esteem, make you happy and healthy
and help you to achieve your relationship and life goals.

Dose: Daily.

How to: Use the 'Over To You' exercise on page 149.

Happy Relationships Rule #6: Achieve Personal Goals

SET REALISTIC, SPECIFIC GOALS

Your objective: To set goals that will make you happy and
healthy within and create happy relationships.

Dose: Do this on Day One of your 4 week plan, and additionally as and when required.

How to: Use the 'Over To You' exercise on page 160.

BOOST MOTIVATION

Your objective: To keep motivation high.

Dose: As and when required.

How to: Use the 'Over To You' exercise on page 163.

Happy Relationships Rule #7: Problem-Solve Relentlessly

USE PROBLEM-SOLVING STRATEGIES

Your objective: To work out the solutions that will get you from your relationship problems to your desired outcomes (from starting point 'A' to desired destination 'B').

Dose: As and when problems arise that you need to resolve to create happy relationships.

How to: Use the 'Over To You' exercise on page 174.

So, keep it simple. Have reminders of your new habits and goals on notes around your home or office, or pinging on your phone, and have specific goals for anything important that you want to achieve and form good habits for.

Keep the Three Pillars of Happy Relationships and the 7 Simple Rules to Create Harmony and Growth handy so that you can ensure you're honouring them and utilising them respectively, and if you're not, work out why not and what you can change to ensure that you do. If, after your best, most sincere efforts, you realise a relationship just isn't good for you, it's important to let it go. Some people are only meant to be in our lives for so long. Mentally thank them for the role they have played, the love and/or the lessons you have received from them, and learn from every relationship so that it becomes easier for you to have happy relationships as the years go by.

Other people are meant to be in our lives forever, and the challenges those relationships bring show you how much you mean to each other and how they develop your strength and character. Mentally and vocally thank them for their love and lessons. Remember to own your worth, whatever you do, and the right people will come into your life, while the wrong ones will slip away. Remember your worth and you'll make great relationship decisions quickly and easily for the rest of your life. Love and look after yourself, and you'll be able to love and look after your loved ones.

Now go and transform your relationships with a simple tweak here and there, so that you can be happy and healthy and have happy relationships!

References

1   Holt-Lunstad, J., Robles, T. F. and Sbarra, D. A. (2017).
    Advancing Social Connection as a Public Health Priority in the
    United States. *American Psychologist*, 72(6): 517–30.

2   Holt-Lunstad, J., Smith, T., Baker, M., Harris, T. and
    Stephenson, D. (2015). Loneliness and Social Isolation as Risk
    Factors for Mortality: A meta-analytic review. *Perspectives on
    Psychological Science*, 10(2): 227–37.

3   Waldinger, R. (2015). What Makes a Good Life? Lessons from
    the longest study on happiness. Ted Talks. Available at: https://
    www.ted.com/talks/robert_waldinger_what_makes_a_good_
    life_lessons_from_the_longest_study_on_happiness/
    transcript?language=en.

4   Stossel, S. (2013). What Makes Us Happy, Revisited. *The Atlantic*.
    Available at: https://www.theatlantic.com/magazine/
    archive/2013/05/thanks-mom/309287/.

5   Fowler, J. H. and Christakis, N. A. (2008). Dynamic Spread of
    Happiness in a Large Social Network: Longitudinal analysis
    over 20 years in the Framingham Heart Study. *BMJ*, 337:a2338.

6   Rosenquist, J. N., Fowler, J. H. and Christakis, N. A. (2011).
    Social Network Determinants of Depression. *Molecular
    Psychiatry*, 16(3): 273–81.

7   Lufityanto, G., Donkin, C. and Pearson, J. (2016). Measuring Intuition: Nonconscious emotional information boosts decision accuracy and confidence. *Psychological Science*, 27(5): 622–34.

8   Voss, J. L. and Paller, K. A. (2009). An Electrophysiological Signature of Unconscious Recognition Memory. *Nature Neuroscience*, 12(3): 349–55.

9   Bechara, A., Damasio, H., Tranel, D. and Damasio, A. R. (1997). Deciding Advantageously Before Knowing the Advantageous Strategy. *Science*, 275(5304): 1293–5.

10 Hodgkinson, G. P., Langan-Fox, J. and Sadler-Smith, E. (2008). Intuition: a fundamental bridging construct in the behavioural sciences. *British Journal of Psychology*, 99(1): 1–27.

11 Collier, L. (2017). Using Objective Data to Improve Performance. *American Psychological Association*, 48(6): 62.

12 Yang, M., Kim, B., Lee, E., Lee, D., Yu, B., Jeon, H. J. and Kim, J. (2014). Worry and Rumination, *Psychiatry and Clinical Neurosciences*, 68(9): 712–20.

13 Shi, X., Brinthaupt, T. M. and McCree, M. (2014). The Relationship of Self-Talk Frequency to Communication Apprehension and Public Speaking Anxiety. *Personality and Individual Differences*, 75: 125–9.

14 Starrs, C., Dunkley, D. and Moroz, M. (2015). Self-Criticism, Low Self-Esteem, Depressive Symptoms, and Eating Disorders. 10.1007/978-981-287-087-2_18-1.

15 Cheng, S.-T., Tsui, P. K. and Lam, J. H. M. (2015). Improving Mental Health in Health Care Practitioners: Randomized controlled trial of a gratitude intervention. *Journal of Consulting and Clinical Psychology*, 83(1): 177–86.

16 Valikhani, A., Ahmadnia, F., Karimi, A. and Mills, P. J. (2019). The Relationship Between Dispositional Gratitude and Quality of Life: The mediating role of perceived stress and mental health. *Personality and Individual Differences*, 141: 40–6.

17 O'Connell, B. H., O'Shea, D. and Gallagher, S. (2016). Mediating Effects of Loneliness on the Gratitude-Health Link. *Personality and Individual Differences*, 98: 179–83.

18 Millstein, R. A., Celano, C. M., Beale, E. E., Beach, S. R., Suarez, L., Belcher, A. M., Januzzi, J. L. and Huffman, J. C. (2016). The Effects of Optimism and Gratitude on Adherence Functioning and Mental Health Following an Acute Coronary Syndrome. *General Hospital Psychiatry*, 43: 17–22.

19 Kini, P., Wong, J., McInnis, S., Gabana, N. and Brown, J. W. (2016). The Effects of Gratitude Expression on Neural Activity. *NeuroImage*, 128: 1–10.

20 Hatziegeorgiadis, A., Zourbanos, N., Mpoumpaki, S. and Theodorakis, Y. (2009). Mechanisms Underlying the Self-Talk-Performance Relationship: The effects of self-talk on self-confidence and anxiety,Psychology of Sport and Exercise, 10(1):186–92.

21 Lane, A. M., Totterdell, P., MacDonald, I., Devonport, T. J., Friesen, A. P., Beedie, C. J. and Nevill, A. (2016). Brief Online Training Enhances Competitive Performance: Findings of the BBC Lab UK Psychological Skills Intervention Study. *Frontiers in Psychology*, 7: 413.

22 Hwang, S., Kim, G., Yang, J. and Yang, E. (2016). The Moderating Effects of Age on the Relationships of Self-Compassion, Self-Esteem, and Mental Health. *Japanese Psychological Research*, 58(2): 194–205.

23   Hulme, N., Hirsch, C. and Stopa, L. (2012). Images of the Self and Self-Esteem: Do positive self-images improve self-esteem in social anxiety? *Cognitive behaviour therapy*, 41(2): 163–173. doi:10.10 80/16506073.2012.664557.

24   Hirsch, C., Meynen, T. and Clark, D. (2010). Negative Self-Imagery in Social Anxiety Contaminates Social Interactions. *Memory*, 12(4): 496–506.

25   Vanman, E. J., Baker, R. and Tobin, S. J. (2018). The Burden of Online Friends: The effects of giving up Facebook on stress and well-being. *The Journal of Social Psychology*, 158(4): 496–508.

26   Minkel, J., Htaik, O., Banks, S. and Dinges, D. (2011). Emotional Expressiveness in Sleep-Deprived Healthy Adults. *Behavioural Sleep Medicine*, 9(1): 5–14.

27   Yoo, S-S., Gujar, N., Hu, P., Jolesz, F. A. and Walker, M. P. (2007). The Human Emotional Brain Without Sleep – a prefrontal amygdala disconnect. *Current Biology*, 17(20): 877–78.

28   Walker, M. P. and van der Helm, E. (2009). Overnight Therapy? The Role of Sleep in Emotional Brain Processing. *Psychological Bulletin*, 135(5): 731–48.

29   Ibid.

30   Cai, D. J., Mednick, S. A., Harrison, E. M., Kanady, J. C. and Mednick, S. C. (2009). REM, Not Incubation, Improves Creativity by Priming Associative Networks. *Proceedings of the National Academy of Sciences*, 106(25): 10130–4; DOI:10.1073/ pnas.0900271106.

31   Harvard Health Publishing. (2009). Sleep and Mental Health. Available at: https://www.health.harvard.edu/newsletter_ article/sleep-and-mental-health.

32 Klumpp, H., Roberts, J., Kapella, M. C., Kennedy, A. E. and Kumar, A. (2017). Subjective and Objective Sleep Quality Modulate Emotion Regulatory Brain Function in Anxiety and Depression. *Depression and Anxiety*, 34(7): 651–60.

33 Baroni, A., Bruzzese, J.-M., Di Bartolo, C. A., Ciarleglio, A. and Shatkin, J. P. (2018). Impact of a Sleep Course on Sleep, Mood and Anxiety Symptoms in College Students: A pilot study. *Journal of American College Health*, 66(1): 41–50; http://doi.org/10 .1080/07448481.2017.1369091.

34 Ochiai, H., Ikei, H., Song, C., Kobayashi, M., Takamatsu, A., Miura, T., Kagawa, T., Li, Q., Kumeda, S., Imai, M. and Miyazaki, Y. (2015). Physiological and Psychological Effects of Forest Therapy on Middle-Aged Males with High-Normal Blood Pressure. *International Journal of Environmental Research and Public Health*, 12: 2532–42. https://doi.org/10.3390/ ijerph120302532.

35 Ochiai, H., Ikei, H., Song, C., Kobayashi, M., Miura, T., Kagawa, T., Miyazaki, Y. (2015). Physiological and Psychological Effects of Forest Therapy Program on Middle-Aged Females. *International Journal of Environmental Research and Public Health*, 12(12): 15222–32. http://doi.org/10.3390/ijerph121214984.

36 Park, S-H. and Mattson, R. H. (2008). Effects of Flowering and Foliage Plants in Hospital Rooms on Patients Recovering from Abdominal Surgery. *HortTechnology*, 18(4): 563–8.

37 Berry, M., Sweeney, M., Morath, J., Odum, A. and Joran, K. (2014). The Nature of Impulsivity: Visual exposure to natural environments decreases impulsive decision-making in a delay discounting task. *PLoS ONE*, 9(5): e97915.

38 Gould van Praag, C. D., Garfinkel, S. N., Sparasci, O., Mees, A., Philippides, A. O., Ware, M., Ottaviani, C. and Critchley, H. D. (2017). Mind-Wandering and Alterations to Default Mode Network Connectivity When Listening to Naturalistic Versus Artificial Sounds. *Scientific Reports*, 7(45273).

39 Saadatmand, V., Rejeh, N., Heravi-Karimooi, M., Tadrisi, S. D., Zayeri, F., Vaismoradi, M. and Jasper, M. (2013). Effect of Nature-Based Sounds' Intervention on Agitation, Anxiety, and Stress in Patients Under Mechanical Ventilator Support: A randomised controlled trial. *International Journal of Nursing Studies*, 50(7): 895–904.

40 Boubekri, M., Cheung, I. N., Reid, K. J., Wang, C. H. and Zee, P. C. (2014). Impact of Windows and Daylight Exposure on Overall Health and Sleep Quality of Office Workers: A case-control pilot study. *Journal of Clinical Sleep Medicine*, 10(6): 603–11.

41 Javani, Z., Madani, R., Hojat, I. and Zadeh, R. (2019). The Relationship Between Daylight and Happiness for Women in Residential Districts of Isfahan, Iran. *Environmental Quality Management*, 28(3): 103–10.

42 Lieberman, M. D., Eisenberger, N. I., Crockett, M. J., Tom, S. M., Pfeifer, J. H., Way, B. M. (2007). Putting Feelings into Words: Affect labeling disrupts amygdala activity in response to affective stimuli. *Psychol Sci.*, 18(5): 421–8.

43 Blumenthal, J. A., Smith, P. J. and Hoffman, B. M. (2012). Is Exercise a Viable Treatment for Depression? *ACSM's Health & Fitness Journal*, 16(4): 14–21.

44 Morres, I. D., Hatzigeorgiadis, A., Stathi, A., Comoutos, N., Arpin-Cribbie, C., Krommidas, C. and Theodorakis, Y. (2018). Aerobic Exercise for Adult Patients with Major Depressive

Disorder in Mental Health Services: A systematic review and meta-analysis. *Depression and Anxiety*, 36(1): 39–53.

45 Cooney, G. M., Dwan, K., Greig, C. A., Lawlor, D. A., Rimer, J., Waugh, F. R., McMurdo, M. and Mead, G. E. (2013). Exercise for Depression. *Cochrane Systematic Review*, 9: CD004366. DOI: 10.1002/14651858.CD004366.pub6.

46 Harvard Health Publishing. (2013). Exercise is an All-Natural Treatment to Fight Depression. Available at: https://www. health.harvard.edu/mind-and-mood/exercise-is-an-al l-natural-treatment-to-fight-depression.

47 Dinoff, A., Herrmann, N., Swardfager, W., Liu, C. S., Sherman, C., Chan, S. and Lanctôt, K. L. (2016). The Effect of Exercise Training on Resting Concentrations of Peripheral Brain-Derived Neurotrophic Factor (BDNF): A meta-analysis. *PLoS ONE*, 11(9), e0163037.

48 Calabrese, F., Rossetti, A. C., Racagni, G., Gass, P., Riva, M. A. and Molteni, R. (2014). Brain-Derived Neurotrophic Factor: A bridge between inflammation and neuroplasticity. *Frontiers in Cellular Neuroscience*, 8: 430.

49 Goldfield, G. S., Kenny, G. P., Alberga, A. S., Prud'homme. D., Hadjiyannakis, S., Gougeon, R. and Sigal, R. J. (2015). Effects of Aerobic training, Resistance Training, or Both on Psychological Health in Adolescents With Obesity: The HEARTY randomized controlled trial. *Journal of Consulting and Clinical Psychology*, 83(6): 1123–35.

50 Herring, M., Jacob, M., Suveg, C., O'Connor, P. J. (2011). Effects of Short-Term Exercise Training on Signs and Symptoms of Generalized Anxiety Disorder. *Mental Health and Physical Activity*, 4: 71–7.

51 Cahn, B. R., Goodman, M. S., Peterson, C. T., Maturi, R. and Mills, P. J. (2017). Yoga, Meditation and Mind-Body Health: Increased BDNF, cortisol awakening response, and altered inflammatory marker expression after a 3-month yoga and meditation retreat. *Frontiers in Human Neuroscience*, 11: 315.

52 Sethi, J. K., Nagendra, H. R. and Ganpat, T. S. (2013). Yoga Improves Attention and Self-Esteem in Underprivileged Girl Student. *Journal of Education and Health Promotion*, 2(55). doi:10.4103/2277-9531.119043.

53 Hölzel, B. K., Carmody, J., Vangel, M., Congleton, C., Yerramsetti, S. M., Gard, T. and Lazar, S. W. (2011). Mindfulness Practice Leads to Increases in Regional Brain Gray Matter Density. *Psychiatry Research: Neuroimaging*, 191(1):36–43.

54 Hölzel, B. K., Carmody, J., Evans, K. C., Hoge, E. A., Dusek, J. A., Morgan, L., Pitman, R. K., and Lazar, S. W. (2009). Stress Reduction Correlates with Structural Changes in the Amygdala. *Social Cognitive and Affective Neuroscience*, 5(1): 11–17.

55 Martelli, A. M., Chester, D. S., Warren Brown, K., Eisenberger, N. I. and DeWall, C. N. (2018). When Less Is More: Mindfulness predicts adaptive affective responding to rejection via reduced prefrontal recruitment. *Social Cognitive and Affective Neuroscience*, 13(6): 648–55.

56 Zhong, C-B. and Liljenquist, K. (2006). Washing Away Your Sins; Threatened morality and physical cleansing. *Science*, 313(5792): 1451–52.

57 Lee, S. and Schwarz, N. (2011). Wiping the Slate Clean: Psychological consequences of physical cleansing. *Current Directions in Psychological Science*, 20(5): 307–11.

58 Lee, S. W. S., Tang, H., Wan, J., Mai, X. and Liu, C. (2015). A
    Cultural Look at Moral Purity: Wiping the face clean. *Frontiers
    in Psychology*, 6: 577.

59 Tang, H., Lu, X., Su, R., Liang, Z., Mai, X. and Liu, C. (2017).
    Washing Away Your Sins in the Brain: Physical cleaning and
    priming of cleaning recruit different brain networks after moral
    threat. *Social Cognitive and Affective Neuroscience*, 12(7): 1149–1158.

60 Ocean, N., Howley, P. and Ensor, J. (2019). Lettuce Be Happy: A
    longitudinal UK study on the relationship between fruit and
    vegetable consumption and well-being. *Social Science &
    Medicine*, 222: 335–45.

61 Agarwal, U., Mishra, S., Xu, J., Levin, S., Gonzales, J. and
    Barnard, N. D. (2014). A Multicenter Randomized Controlled
    Trial of a Nutrition Intervention Program in a Multiethnic
    Adult Population in the Corporate Setting Reduces Depression
    and Anxiety and Improves Quality of Life: The GEICO Study.
    American Journal of Health Promotion, 29(4): 245–54.

62 Foster, J. A. and McVey Neufeld, K.-A. (2013). Gut-Brain Axis:
    How the microbiome influences anxiety and depression. *Trends
    in Neurosciences*, 36(5): 305–12.

63 Khayyat, Y. and Attar, S. (2015). Vitamin D Deficiency in
    Patients with Irritable Bowel Syndrome: Does it exist? *Oman
    Medical Journal*, 30(2): 115–18.

64 Penckofer, S., Kouba, J., Byrn, M. and Ferrans, C. E. (2011).
    Vitamin D and Depression: Where is all the sunshine? *Issues
    Mental Health Nursing*, 31(6): 385–93.

65   Quoidbach, J., Gross, J. J. and Mikolajczak, M. (2015). Positive
     Interventions: An emotion regulation perspective. *Psychological
     Bulletin*, 141(3):655–93

66   Cook, E. and Chater, A. (2013). Are Happier People, Healthier
     People? The relationship between perceived happiness, personal
     control, BMI and health preventive behaviours. *International
     Journal of Health Promotion and Education*, 48(2): 58–64.

67   Galatzer-Levy, I. R., Brown, A. D., Henn-Haase, C., Metzler, T.
     J., Neylan, T. C. and Marmar, C. R. (2013). Positive and
     Negative Emotion Prospectively Predict Trajectories of
     Resilience and Distress Among High-Exposure Police Officers.
     Emotion, 13(3): 545–53.

68   Hoppmann, C. A., Gerstorf, D., Willis, S. L. and Schaie, K. W.
     (2011). Spousal Interrelations in Happiness in the Seattle
     Longitudinal Study: Considerable similarities in levels and
     change over time. *Developmental Psychology*, 47(1): 1–8.

69   Maher, A. C., Kielb, S., Loyer, E., Connelley, M., Rademaker, A.,
     Mesulam, M.-M., Weintraub, S., McAdams, D., Logan, R. and
     Rogalski, E. (2017) Psychological Well-Being in Elderly Adults
     with Extraordinary Episodic Memory. *PLoS ONE*, 12(10):
     e0186413.

70   Condon, P., Desbordes, G., Desteno, D. and Miller, W. B. (2013).
     Meditation Increases Compassionate Responses to Suffering.
     Psychological Science, 24(10).

71   Shapiro, S. L., Brown, K. W. and Biegel, G. M. (2007). Teaching
     Self-Care to Caregives: Effects of mindfulness-based stress
     reduction on the mental health of therapists in training.
     Training and Education in Professional Psychology, 1(2): 105–115.

72 McKay, S. (2012). Carnegie Foundation. Using New Research to Improve Student Motivation. Available at: https://www.carnegiefoundation.org/blog/using-new-research-to-improve-student-motivation/.

73 Gere, J. and Impett, E. A. (2017). Shifting Priorities: Effects of partners' goal conflict on goal adjustment processes and relationship quality in developing romantic relationships. *Journal of Social and Personal Relationships*, 35(6): 793–810.

74 Assad, K. K., Brent, D. M. and Conger, R. D. (2007). Optimism: An enduring resource for romantic relationships. *Journal of Personality and Social Psychology*, 93(2): 285–97.

75 Thompson, C. M., Romo, L. K. and Dailey, R. M. (2013). The Effectiveness of Weight Management Influence Messages in Romantic Relationships. *Communication Research Reports*, 30(1): 34–45.

76 Ahmad, M. H., Shahar, S., Teng, N. I., Manaf, Z. A., Sakian, N. I. and Omar, B. (2014). Applying Theory of Planned Behavior to Predict Exercise Maintenance in Sarcopenic Elderly. *Clinical Interventions in Aging*, 9: 1551–61

77 Sheppard, B. H., Hartwick, J. and Warshaw, P. R. (1988). The Theory of Reasoned Action: A meta-analysis of past research with recommendations for modifications and future research. *Journal of Consumer Research*, 15(3): 325–43.

78 Tarkiainen, A. and Sundqvist, S. (2005). Subjective Norms, Attitudes and Intentions of Finnish Consumers in Buying Organic Food. *British Food Journal*, 107(11): 808–22.

79   Algoe, S. B., Gable, S. L. and Maisel, N. C. (2010). It's the Little Things: Everyday gratitude as a booster shot for romantic relationships. *Personal Relationships*, 17(2): 217–33.

80   Bao, K. J. and Lyubomirsky, S. (2013). Making It Last: Combating hedonic adaption in romantic relationships. *The Journal of Positive Psychology*, 8(3): 196–206.

81   Bello, R. S., Brandau-Brown, F. E., Zhang, S. and Ragsdale, J. D. (2010). Verbal and Nonverbal Methods for Expressing Appreciation in Friendships and Romantic Relationships: A cross-cultural comparison. *International Journal of Intercultural Relations*, 34(3): 294–302.

82   Croft, A., Dunn, E. W. and Quoidbach, J. (2012). From Tribulations to Appreciation: Experiencing adversity in the past predicts greater savoring in the present. *Social Psychological and Personality Science*, 5(5): 511–6.

83   Poulin, M. J. and Haase, C. M. (2015). Growing to Trust: Evidence that trust increases and sustains well-being across the life span. *Social Psychological and Personality Science*, 6(6): 614–21.

84   Zak, P. J. (2018). The Neuroscience of High-Trust Organizations. *Consulting Psychology Journal: Practice and Research*, 70(1): 45–58.

85   Riedl, R. and Javor, A. (2012). The Biology of Trust: Integrating evidence from genetics, endocrinology, and functional brain imaging. *Journal of Neuroscience, Psychology, and Economics*, 5(2): 63–91.

86   Edwards, S. (2015). Love and the Brain. *Harvard Mahoney Neuroscience Institute*, available at: https://neuro.hms.harvard.edu/harvard-mahoney-neuroscience-institute/brain-newsletter/and-brain-series/love-and-brain.

87 Uysal, A., Lin, H. L. and Bush, A. L. (2012). The Reciprocal Cycle of Self-Concealment and Trust in Romantic Relationships. *European Journal of Social Psychology*, 42(7): 844–51.

88 Sarkis, S. A. (2017). 11 Warning Signs of Gaslighting. *Psychology Today*, available at: psychologytoday.com/gb/blog/here-ther e-and-everywhere/201701/11-warning-signs-gaslighting.

89 Babiak, P., Neumann, C. S. and Hare, R. D. (2010). Corporate Psychopathy: Talking the walk. *Behavioural Sciences and the Law*, 28:174–93. Available at: https://www.sakkyndig.com/psykologi/ artvit/babiak2010.pdf.

90 Hirstein, W. (2017). 9 Clues That You May Be Dealing with A Psychopath. *Psychology Today*, available at: https://www. psychologytoday.com/intl/blog/mindmelding/201706/9-clue s-you-may-be-dealing-psychopath.

91 Neal, A. M. and Lemay, E. P. (2017). The Wandering Eye Perceives More Threats: Projection of attraction to alternative partners predicts anger and negative behavior in romantic relationships. *Journal of Social and Personal Relationships*, 36(2): 450–68.

92 Aknin, L. B., Broesch, T., Hamlin, J. K. and Van de Vondervoort, J. W. (2015). Prosocial Behavior Leads to Happiness in a Small-Scale Rural Society. *Journal of Experimental Psychology: General*, 144(4): 788–95.

93 Piferi, R. L. and Lawler, K. A. (2006). Social Support and Ambulatory Blood Pressure: An examination of both receiving and giving. *International Journal of Psychophysiology*, 62(2): 328–36.

94 Alessi, E. J. (2016). Resilience in Sexual and Gender Minority Forced Migrants: A qualitative exploration. *Traumatology*, 22(3).

95   Kelly, S. D., Kravitz, C. and Hopkins, M. (2003). Neural
     Correlates of Bimodal Speech and Gesture Comprehension.
     Brain and Language, 89(1): 253–60.

96   Newberg, A., and Waldman, M. R. (2012). *Words Can Change
     Your Brain: 12 Conversation Strategies to Build Trust, Resolve
     Conflict, and Increase Intimacy*, New York: Avery.

97   Pell, M. D., Rothermich, K., Liu, P., Paulmann, S., Sethi, S. and
     Rigoulot, S. (2015). Preferential Decoding of Emotion from
     Human Non-Linguistic Vocalizations Versus Speech Prosody.
     Biological Psychology, 111: 14–25.

98   Heart Math Institute (2012). Heart Intelligence. Available at:
     https://www.heartmath.org/articles-of-the-heart/
     the-math-of-heartmath/heart-intelligence.

99   Feng, S., Suri, R. and Bell, M. (2014). Does Classical Music
     Relieve Math Anxiety? Role of tempo on price computation
     avoidance. *Psychology & Marketing*, 31: 489–99.

100 Ibid.

101 Panteleeva, Y., Ceschi, G., Glowinski, D., Courvoisier, D. S. and
     Grandjean, D. (2017). Music for Anxiety? Meta-analysis of
     anxiety reduction in non-clinical samples. *Psychology of Music*,
     46(4): 473–87.

102 Murcia, C. Q., Kreutz, G., Clift, S. and Bongard, S. (2010). Shall
     We Dance? An exploration of the perceived benefits of dancing
     on well-being. *Arts & Health*, 2(2): 149–63.

103 Powell, A. (2012). Decoding keys to a healthy life. Available at:
     https://news.harvard.edu/gazette/story/2012/02/decoding-key
     s-to-a-healthy-life/.

104 Aaron, R. E., Rinehart, K. and Ceballos, N. (2011). Arts-Based Interventions to Reduce Anxiety Levels Among College Students. *Arts & Health*, 3: 27–28.

105 Sandmire, D., Gorham, S., Rankin, N. and Grimm, D. (2012). The Influence of Art Making on Anxiety: A pilot study. *Art Therapy*, 29(2): 68–73.

106 Triantoro, S. and Yunita, A. (2014). The Efficacy of Art Therapy to Reduce Anxiety Among Bullying Victims. *International Journal of Research Studies in Psychology*, 3:10.5861/ijrsp.2014.829.

107 Nichols, N. B., Backer-Fulghum, L. M., Boska, C. R. and Sanford, K. (2015). Two Types of Disengagement During Couples' Conflicts: Withdrawal and passive immobility. *Psychological Assessment*, 27(1): 203–14.

108 Haase, C. M., Holley, S. R., Bloch, L., Verstaen, A. and Levenson, R. W. (2016). Interpersonal Emotional Behaviors and Physical Health: A 20-year longitudinal study of long-term married couples. *Emotion*, 16(7): 965–77.

109 Hicks, A. M. and Diamond, L. M. (2011). Don't Go to Bed Angry: Attachment, conflict, and affective and physiological reactivity. *Personal Relationships*, 18(2): 266–84.

110 Doidge, N. (2008). *The Brain That Changes Itself: Stories of personal triumph from the frontiers of brain science*, London: Penguin.

111 Pascual-Leone, A., Amedi, A., Fregni, F. and Merabet, L. B. (2005). The Plastic Human Brain Cortex. *Annual Review of Neuroscience*, 28: 377–401.

112 van Lankveld, J., Jacobs, N., Thewissen, V., Dewitte, M. and Verboon, P. (2018). The Associations of Intimacy and Sexuality in Daily Life: Temporal dynamics and gender effects within romantic relationships. *Journal of Social and Personal Relationships*, 35(4): 557–76.

113 Kito, M. (2010). Self-Disclosure in Romantic Relationships and Friendships Among American and Japanese College Students. *Journal of Social Psychology*, 145(2): 127–40.

114 Roberts, J. A. and David, M. E. (2016). My Life Has Become A Major Distraction from My Cell Phone: Partner phubbing and relationship satisfaction among romantic partners. *Computers in Human Behavior*, 54: 134–41.

115 Clayton, R. B. (2014). The Third Wheel: The impact of Twitter use on relationship infidelity and divorce. *Cyberpsychology, Behavior, and Social Networking*, 17(7): 425–30.

116 Field, T., Hernandez-Reif, M., Diego, M., Schanberg, S. and Kuhn, C. (2005). Cortisol Decreases and Serotonin and Dopamine Increase Following Massage Therapy. *International Journal of Neuroscience*, 115(10): 1397–1413.

117 Magnon, N. and Kalra, S. (2011). The Orgasmic History of Oxytocin: Love, lust and labor. *Indian Journal of Endocrinology and Metabolism*, 15(3): 156–61.

118 Gobrogge, K. and Wang, Z. (2016). The Ties That Bond: Neurochemistry of attachment in voles. *Current Opinion in Neurobiology*, 38: 80–8.

119 Algoe, S. B., Kurtz, L. E. and Grewen, K. (2017). Oxytocin and Social Bonds: The role of oxytocin in perceptions of romantic partners' bonding behavior. *Psychological Science*, 28(12): 1763–72.

120 Ditzen, B., Schaer, M., Gabriel, B. and Bodenmann, G. (2008). Intranasal Oxytocin Increases Positive Communication and Reduces Cortisol Levels During Couple Conflict. *Biological Psychiatry*, 65(9): 728–31.

121 Hertenstein, M. J., Holmes, R., McCullogh, M. and Keltner, D. (2009). The Communication of Emotion Via Touch. *Emotion*, 9(4): 566–73.

122 Hertenstein, M. J. and Keltner, D. (2011). Gender and the Communication of Emotion Via Touch. *Sex Roles*, 64(1-2): 70–80.

123 Hietanen, J. K. (2018). Affective Eye Contact: An integrative review. *Frontiers in Psychology*, 9: 1587.

124 Farroni, T., Csibra, G., Simion, F. and Johnson, M. H. (2002). Eye Contact Detection in Humans from Birth. *Proceedings of the National Academy of Sciences of the United States of America*, 99(14): 9602–5.

125 Bateson, M., Nettle, D. and Roberts, G. (2006). Cues of Being Watched Enhance Cooperation in a Real-World Setting. *Biology Letters*, 2(3): 412–4.

126 Ernest-Jones, M., Nettle, D. and Bateson, M. (2011). Effects of Eye Images on Everyday Cooperative Behavior: A field experiment. *Evolution and Human Behavior*, 32(3): 172–8.

127 Kreysa, H., Kessler, L. and Schweinberger, S. R. (2016). Direct Speaker Gaze Promotes Trust in Truth-Ambiguous Statements. *PLoS One*, 11(9): e0162291.

128 Kret, M. E., Fischer, A. H. and De Dreu, C. K. W. (2015). Pupil Mimicry Correlates with Trust in In-Group Partners With Dilating Pupils. *Psychological Science*, 26(9): 1401–10.

129 Kret, M. E. and De Dreu, C. K. W. (2019). The Power of Pupil Size in Establishing Trust and Reciprocity. *Journal of Experimental Psychology: General*, 148(8): 1299–311.

130 Lee, D. H. and Anderson, A. K. (2017). Reading What the Mind Thinks from How the Eye Sees. *Psychological Science*, 28(4): 494–503.

131 Leavitt, C. E. and Willoughby, B. J. (2015). Associations Between Attempts at Physical Intimacy and Relational Outcomes Among Cohabiting and Married Couples. *Journal of Social and Personal Relationships*, 32(2): 241–62.

132 Impett, E. A., Strachman, A., Finkel, E. J. and Gable, S. L. (2008). Maintaining Sexual Desire in Intimate Relationships: The importance of approach goals. *Journal of Personality and Social Psychology*, 94(5): 808–23.

133 Yeh, H.-C., Loenz, F. O., Wickrama, K. A. S., Conger, R. D. and Elder, G. H., Jr. (2006). Relationships Among Sexual Satisfaction, Marital Quality, and Marital Instability at Midlife. *Journal of Family Psychology*, 20(2): 339–43.

134 Meltzer, A. L., Makhanova, A., Hicks, L. L., French, J. E., McNulty, J. K. and Bradbury, T. N. (2017). Quantifying the Sexual Afterglow: The lingering benefits of sex and their implications for pair-bonded relationships. *Psychological Science*, 28(5): 587–98.

135 McDaniel, B. T., Drouin, M. and Cravens, J. D. (2017). Do You Have Anything to Hide? Infidelity-related behaviors on social media sites and marital satisfaction. *Computers in Human Behavior*, 66: 88–95.

136 Muise, A., Harasymchuk, C., Day, L. S., Bacev-Giles, C., Gere, J. and Impett, E. A. (2019). Broadening Your Horizons: Self-expanding activities promote desire and satisfaction in established romantic relationships. *Journal of Personality and Social Psychology*, 116(2): 237–58.

137 Emery, L. F. and Le, B. (2014). Imagining the White Picket Fence: Social class, future plans, and romantic relationship quality. *Social Psychological and Personality Science*, 5(6): 653–61.

138 Hadden, B. W. and Knee, C. R. (2016). Finding Meaning in Us: The role of meaning in life and romantic relationships. *The Journal of Positive Psychology*, 13(3): 226–39.

139 Heart Math Institute (2012). Heart Intelligence. Available at: https://www.heartmath.org/articles-of-the-heart/ the-math-of-heartmath/heart-intelligence.

140 NIH. How the Heart Works: The heart's electrical system. Available at: https://www.nhlbi.nih.gov/node/3725.

141 McCraty, R. (2017). New Frontiers in Heart Rate Variability and Social Coherence Research: Techniques, technologies, and implications for improving group dynamics and outcomes. *Frontiers in Public Health*, 5: 267

142 McCraty, R., Deyhle, A. and Childre, D. (2012). The Global Coherence Initiative: Creating a coherent planetary standing wave. *Global Advances in Health and Medicine*, 1(1): 64–77.

143 Morris, S. (2010). Achieving Collective Coherence: Group effects on heart rate variability coherence and heart rhythm synchronization. *Alternative Therapies*, 16(4).

144 Konvalinka, I., Xygalatas, D., Bulbulia, J., Schjødt, U., Jegindø, E-M., Wallot, E., Van Orden, G. and Roepstorff, A. (2011). Synchronized Arousal Between Performers and Related Spectators in a Fire-Walking Ritual. *Proceedings of the National Academy of Sciences*, 108(20): 8524–9.

145 Ferrer, E. and Helm, J. (2012). Dynamical Systems Modeling of Physiological Coregulation in Dyadic Interactions. *International Journal of Psychophysiology*, 88(3): 296–308.

146 Mitkidis, P., McGraw, J., Roepstorff, A. and Wallot, S. (2015). Building Trust: Heart rate synchrony and arousal during joint action increased by public goods game. *Physiology & Behavior*, 149: 101–6.

147 McCraty, R., Atkinson, M. and Bradley, R. T. (2004). Electrophysiological Evidence of Intuition: Part 1. The surprising role of the heart. *Journal of Alternative and Complementary Medicine*, 10(1): 133–43.

148 Rezaei, S., Mirzaei, M. and Zali, M. R. (2014). Nonlocal Intuition: Replication and paired-subjects enhancement effects. *Global Advances in Health and Medicine*, 3(2): 5–15.

149 McCraty, R. and Atkinson, M. (2014). Electrophysiology of Intuition: Pre-stimulus responses in group and individual participants using a roulette paradigm. *Global Advances in Health and Medicine*, 3(2): 16–27.

150 Valenzuela, S., Halpern, D. and Katz, J. (2014). Social Network Sites, Marriage Well-Being and Divorce: Survey and state-level evidence from the United States. *Computers in Human Behavior*, 36: 94–101.

151 Clayton, R., Nagurney, A. and Smith, J. (2013). Cheating, Breakup and Divorce: Is Facebook use to blame? *Cyberpsychology, Behavior, and Social Networking,* 16(10): 717–20.

152 Parker, F. (2017). Excessive Use of Social Media is Now Being Used as a Reason For Divorce. *Metro,* available at: https://metro.co.uk/2017/05/19/excessive-use-of-social-media-is-now-being-used-as-a-reason-for-divorce-6648183/.

153 Vendemia, M. A., High, A. and DeAndrea, D. (2017). "Friend" or Foe? Why people friend disliked others on facebook. *Communications Research Reports,* 34: 29–36.

154 Abbasi, I. S. (2018). Falling Prey to Online Romantic Alternatives: Evaluating social media alternative partners in committed versus dating relationships. *Social Science Computer Review,* https://doi.org/10.1177/0894439318793947.

155 Gollwitzer, P. M. and Brandstatter, V. (1997). Implementation Intentions and Effective Goal Pursuit. *Journal of Personality and Social Psychology,* 73(1): 186–99.

156 Locke, E. A. and Latham, G. P. (2002). Building a Practically Useful Theory of Goal Setting and Task Motivation: A 35-year odyssey. *American Psychologist,* 57(9): 705–17.

157 Ehrsson, H. H., Geyer, S. and Naito, E. (2003). Imagery of Voluntary Movement of Fingers, Toes and Tongue Activates Corresponding Body-Part-Specific Motor Representations. *Journal of Neurophysiology,* 90(5): 3304–16

158 Lyubomirsky, S. and Layous, K. (2013). How Do Simple Positive Activities Increase Well-Being? *Current Directions in Psychological Science,* 22(1): 57–62.

159 Osborn, A. (1953). *Applied Imagination: Principles and Procedures of Creative Problem-Solving*, New York: Creative Education and Foundation Press.

160 Soon, C. S., Brass, M., Heinze, H. J. and Haynes, J. D. (2008). Unconscious Determinants of Free Decisions in the Human Brain. *Nature Neuroscience*, 11(5): 543–5.

161 Oppezzo, M. and Schwartz, D. L. (2014). Give Your Idea Some Legs: The positive effect of walking on creative thinking. *Journal of Experimental Psychology: Learning, Memory, and Cognition*, 40(4): 1142–52.

162 Christoff, K., Gordon, A. M., Smallwood, J., Smith, R. and Schooler, J. W. (2009). Experience Sampling During fMRI Reveals Default Network and Executive System Contributions to Mind Wandering. *Proceedings of the National Academy of Sciences of the United States of America*, 106(21): 8719–24.

163 Cai, D. J., Mednick, S. A., Harrison, E. M., Kanady, J. C. and Mednick, S. C. (2009). 'REM, Not Incubation, Improves Creativity by Priming Associative Networks. *Proceedings of the National Academy of Sciences*, 106(25): 10130–4; DOI:10.1073/pnas.090027110.

164 Horne, J. A. (1988). Sleep Loss and "Divergent" Thinking Ability. *Sleep*, 11(6):528–36.

165 Beijamini, F., Pereira, S. I. R., Cini, F. A. and Louzada, F. M. (2014). After Being Challenged by a Video Game Problem, Sleep Increases the Chance to Solve It. *PLoS ONE*, 9(1): e84342.

166 Isen, A. M., Daubman, K.A. and Nowicki, G. P. (1987). Positive Affect Facilitates Creative Problem Solving. *Journal of Personality and Social Psychology*, 52(6): 1122–31.

Acknowledgements

I am so incredibly grateful to all the team at Orion Publishing who made this journey possible, who helped me to create the end results with all three books in this series, *Resilient Me*, *Anxiety Free* and *Happy Relationships*.

I also wouldn't be here if it weren't for my lovely talent agent and my book agent who understand me effortlessly, know how to get the best out of me, and are always there for me.

Then there are my clients who have allowed me to share their journeys with them, and their stories (with names changed, of course).

I also want to thank all the people in my life who have affirmed my worth, appreciated me, empowered me, loved me, and taught me how important human relationships are.

And I want to thank you, my readers, because your belief in me and the kind words you have shared, have made this whole process of writing and publishing three books in three years, worth it beyond words.

Thank you so, so much, everyone. xx